THE ROAD TO VICTORY

THE UNTOLD STORY OF WORLD WAR II'S RED BALL EXPRESS

THE ROAD TO VICTORY

THE UNTOLD STORY OF WORLD WAR II'S RED BALL EXPRESS

DAVID COLLEY

BRASSEY'S
WASHINGTON, D.C.

Library of Congress Cataloging-in-Publication Data

Colley, David.
   The road to victory : the untold story of World War II's Red Ball Express / David Colley.—1st ed.
      p. cm.
   Includes bibliographical references and index.
      1. World War, 1939–1945—Transportation. 2. World War, 1939–1945—Equipment and supplies. 3. World War, 1939–1945—Afro-Americans. 4. World War, 1939–1945—Campaigns—Western Front. I. Title
D810.T8 C65 2000
940.54′21—dc21   99-048012

ISBN 1-57488-173-6 (alk. paper)

Printed in the United States of America on acid-free paper that meets the American National Standards Institute Z39-48 Standard.

Brassey's
22841 Quicksilver Drive
Dulles, Virginia 20166

First Edition

10 9 8 7 6 5 4 3 2 1

Dedicated to the members of C and I Companies, 514th QM Truck Regiment, and the hundreds of thousands of African American soldiers whose service during World War II has never been fully recognized by the nation for which they served in the cause of equality and justice.

And to Mary Liz

CONTENTS

Map 1: HIGHWAY EXPRESS ROUTES

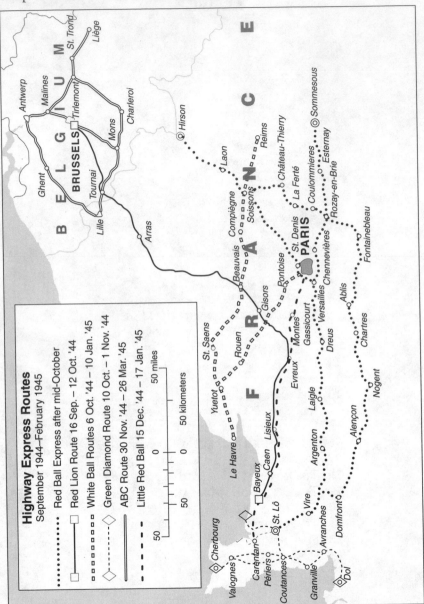

Highway Express Routes
September 1944–February 1945

- ⚬⚬⚬ Red Ball Express after mid-October
- ☐━━☐ Red Lion Route 16 Sep. – 12 Oct. '44
- ▫▫▫ White Ball Routes 6 Oct. '44 – 10 Jan. '45
- ◇╌╌◇ Green Diamond Route 10 Oct. – 1 Nov. '44
- ━━━ ABC Route 30 Nov. '44 – 26 Mar. '45
- ▬ ▬ ▬ Little Red Ball 15 Dec. '44 – 17 Jan. '45

50 miles
50 kilometers
50   0   50
50   0   50

Map 2: ROUTES OF THE RED BALL EXPRESS

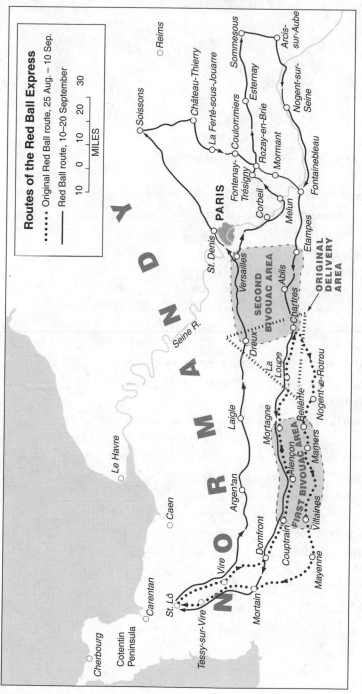

Routes of the Red Ball Express

········· Original Red Ball route, 25 Aug. – 10 Sep.

——— Red Ball route, 10–20 September

MILES

10   0   10   20   30

ILLUSTRATIONS

ACKNOWLEDGEMENTS

I am indebted to former members of C Company, 514th Truck Regiment, who gathered one Saturday afternoon at the home of James Rookard in Cleveland, Ohio, to bring life to the story of the Red Ball Ball Express and the black quartermaster trucking companies that served in the European Theater of Operations in 1944 and 1945. Besides Rookard, Jack Blackwell, James Chappelle, Marvin Hall, Napoleon Hendricks, and Herman Heard took time to remember those long-ago days in France.

I interviewed several other members of C Company by telephone: James Bailey, of Dayton, Ohio, and Charles Fletcher and Fred Newton, both of the Cleveland area. Unfortunately, Fletcher and Newton died before the rest of the group assembled for the interview. I also interviewed John Houston, of Fort Lee, N.J., several times by telephone. He too was a member of C Company.

The U.S. Army Military History Institute in Carlisle, Pa., was a major source of material for this book. Librarians John Slonaker and Louise Arnold Friend were especially helpful. I wish to thank the staff of the Easton (Pa.) Area Public Library for their help, Dorothy Patoki of Interlibrary loan, in particular, and the staff of the Lafayette College Library in Easton.

The U.S. Army Transportation Museum at Fort Eustis, Va., also made valuable information available, as did the National Archives. Timothy K. Henninger, with the Technical Reference

Branch of the National Archives, was exceedingly helpful in retrieving material relating to the Red Ball.

Special thanks go to Bob Rubino and Frank Buck of The Motor Pool in Bartonsville, Pa. They made their knowledge of World War II military vehicles, as well as a restored 1941 Jimmy, available to me. Lee Holland of Virginia and Bryce Sunderlin of Michigan also provided their knowledge about the workings of the Jimmy.

This book could not have been possible without the help of editor Stanley Parkhill of CAM magazine, who contracted for an article on the Red Ball. Later research led to this book.

Fall 1944—somewhere in eastern France at dusk, a jeep carrying a first lieutenant in charge of a platoon of trucks hauling supplies to the front crested a hill. The young officer instinctively scanned the horizon for German aircraft that sometimes swooped in low on strafing runs. The sky was empty, and as far as the eye could see ahead and to the rear, the descending night was hauntingly pierced by the headlights of hundreds of trucks snaking along the highway.

The lengthy convoy, stretching away to the horizons, was part of the Red Ball Express, the legendary military trucking operation in the European Theater of Operations (ETO) in World War II that operated around the clock and supplied the rapidly advancing American armies as they streamed toward Germany. The Red Ball was a critical part of the tidal wave of arms, men, and machines that overwhelmed the German armies. Today, it goes largely unheralded by a postwar generation, but veterans of the ETO remember the Red Ball with pride, respect, and some amusement as they recall the trucks racing to the front with essential supplies, particularly gasoline.

Without the Red Ball and the sister military express trucking lines that it spawned later in the war, World War II in the ETO undoubtedly would have been prolonged and the extraordinary mobility of the American Army drastically limited. Certainly, the Red Ball contributed significantly to the defeat of the German Army in France during the summer and fall of 1944.

The Army organized the Red Ball Express on 25 August 1944, to rush supplies to the rapidly advancing First and Third American Armies when the German Seventh and Fifth Panzer Armies began to disintegrate and retreat eastward toward the German frontier. The French rail system west of Paris had been bombed to shambles, and the Germans held most of the French ports. The only method of supply for the Americans was to transport materiel by truck from the invasion beaches to the front.

So desperate were the Americans to catch and destroy the enemy after the breakout from the Normandy bridgehead two months after D-Day that only the most critical supplies—ammunition, rations, medical supplies, and gasoline—were being hauled. The materiel was transported largely by thousands of six-by-six, 2½-ton General Motors trucks, affectionately nicknamed "Jimmies." The spearheading armored divisions, with their tanks, half-tracks, trucks, and jeeps, couldn't run without fuel. The infantry needed rations, ammunition, and transport into battle, and the artillery needed shells.

The Red Ball Express lasted eighty-one days, from 25 August through 16 November 1944. By the end of those three months, the Red Ball had established itself firmly in the mythology of World War II. More than six thousand trucks and trailers and some twenty-three thousand men transported 412,193 tons of supplies to the advancing American armies from Normandy to the German frontier.

Red Ball became the "tail" of an American Army that was the most highly mechanized and mobile combat force the world had ever seen. The Red Ball route ran from the beaches of Normandy and the ports of the Cotentin Peninsula, principally Cherbourg, to Paris, 270 miles to the east. From Paris, it branched to Verdun and Metz in the southeast, and to Hirson in northeast France on the frontier with Belgium.

Even the Germans, who had developed the blitzkrieg in their lightning invasions of Poland, the Low Countries, and France in

1939 and 1940, were astonished by the speed and mobility of the American advance, particularly that led by Gen. George S. Patton, and by the unimaginable number of vehicles and trucks that supplied the American forces.

What is most often overlooked about the Red Ball operation, as well as the war in Europe, is the contribution made by the African American soldiers assigned to Quartermaster and Transportation Corps units. Although three-fourths of Red Ball drivers were black, and the majority of the quartermaster truck companies in the ETO were manned by blacks, African American troops represented less than 10 percent of all military personnel in World War II. When the call went out to form the Red Ball Express, African American troops, in large measure, kept the supply lines rolling.

The Red Ball formed the basis of several later express routes with different designations, some for specific tasks, that operated through the rest of the war. The largest of these was the XYZ line that transported supplies to U.S. forces advancing across Germany during the spring of 1945.

The Red Ball was retired on 16 November 1944, when its usefulness declined because the Allied armies were stalled by tenacious enemy forces at the German frontier. But Red Ball never really died. Its name and mystique were so embedded in the mythology of World War II that, even after its termination, most of the men who drove the trucks until the end of the war believed that they were part of the Red Ball. Welby Frantz, a trucking company commander who later became president of the American Trucking Association and whose unit did not arrive in France from Iran until February 1945, still believed, a half century after the war, that his unit was on the Red Ball. "That's what we were all told."[1]

Some of the confusion came about because the Transportation Corps shoulder patch, issued to the men in the trucking companies in 1945, carried a red sphere centered on a yellow background shield. Most soldiers who wore the patch assumed that it meant they were on the Red Ball.

The average GI, then and now, often refers to all trucking operations in the ETO—indeed, the entire motorized transport system—as the Red Ball Express. Frank Buergler, a sergeant with an engineering battalion in the 94th Division, remembered a section of autobahn, deep inside Germany toward the end of the war, being marked with splotches of red paint to direct traffic forward. "Oh, it was the Red Ball," he says. To the Americans in the ETO, there was only one trucking line to the front—the Red Ball Express.[2]

The Red Ball was so much a part of World War II in the ETO that it was the subject of a movie, *The Red Ball Express*, starring Jeff Chandler and Sidney Poitier, in 1952. Even though the film bore little resemblance to the real Red Ball, it acclaimed the express line for its role in winning the war.

A Broadway revue, *Call Me Mister*, starring Melvin Douglas and staged in 1946, literally sang the praises of the Red Ball Express:

There are songs of infantry, of the air corps and the sea,
Of the coast guard and Marines in battle dress.
We sing August forty-four and the Normandy shore,
Just the story of the old RED BALL EXPRESS.

Driving truck loads night and day, thirty-six hours on the way,
They supplied our hungry armies from the shore.
Steam was hissing from our hoods, when they showed up with the goods,
But they turned around and went right back for more.

In a never-ending chain, thru the mud and thru the rain,
Closing up the gaps the shells left in their file,
They kept driving, holding tight, sometimes stopped to dig and fight.
They high-balled on, a song for every mile.

Oh, the way their trucks did hop, would have killed a traffic cop.
There was driving out of this world on those runs.
Sometimes one truck would detour, draw the fire—to make sure
That the other loads got safely by the guns.

So we sing this ballad for the old quartermaster corps,
Just a small part of the team of victory.
Tho you may not know the name, there are plenty all the same,
Never will forget that job in Normandy.

To this very day they say, when the night is dull and gray,
Norman farmers hear a strange hullabaloo,
And they peep outside and yell, French for "shut my mouth; do tell,"
As a ghostly car-a-van comes bouncing thru!

It's the RED BALL EXPRESS roaring by!
It's the RED BALL EXPRESS roaring by—
With one man at the wheel and one man at the gun
And a pride in the job to be done.
With the clash of gears and the clanking of chains,
And a song ringing clear to the sky.
It's the RED BALL EXPRESS roaring by, roaring by. . . .[3]

This book focuses on the "official" Red Ball Express that ran from August to November 1944 and, in so doing, relates the critical role played by the operation's trucks and drivers in winning the war.

A generation after World War II, Col. John D. Eisenhower, a veteran of the European war and son of Supreme Commander Dwight D. Eisenhower, paid as much tribute to the men who drove the Red Ball trucks as to those who drove the tanks. Eisenhower wrote in his history, *The Bitter Woods*: "Without it [Red Ball] the advance across France could not have been made."[4]

A FOOTHOLD
IN NORMANDY

Pfc. James Rookard strained to see beyond the landing craft ramp as it rattled and clanked down in deep surf off the Normandy coast of France in early July 1944. As the metallic racket ceased, an eerie silence followed, broken only by the forceful lapping of the sea against the vessel. Rookard had hoped to see more definition where water ended and land began but perceived only endless darkness. The basalt-black waters of the English Channel were invisible in the moonless night, and the sea could be discerned only by the luminous froth of breaking waves hissing on an invisible shoreline. Rookard had expected a more tumultuous introduction to war, but he looked out on a world that was quiet and strangely calm. As shadowy figures of Navy seamen darted about the landing craft and readied the trucks for departure, Rookard gripped the steering wheel of a 2½-ton General Motors Corporation (GMC) truck and waited for the order to move into the night.

Reality suddenly overtook this eighteen-year-old black soldier from Cleveland, Ohio. It had been a year and a half since he was a high school kid who had set out for Camp Hays in Columbus after being inducted into the Army. Rookard remembered the months of training; the drudgery, the anxiety, and the boredom in Stateside military outposts; and the rage induced by racial taunts and insults. Mercifully, his unit had been shipped to England in early 1944 where camp life had been good, even while the training was hard and relentless. The English had been kind and color-blind to the men of Rookard's all-black unit, and American whites, with their prejudices, were kept away from the rural village where he and his comrades were based. Now, that all seemed a lifetime away as the landing craft bobbed in the channel surf. Rookard took a deep breath and waited. He would soon be at war.

The black sergeant at Rookard's side, Jack Blackwell, was a lifer compared to Rookard. Conscripted in 1940 in the peacetime draft, Blackwell had been in the Army for four years. Without regard to the darkness that enveloped the coast of France, Blackwell ordered Rookard to drive on, and the six-wheel–drive vehicle lurched forward, across the deck, and down the ramp into the water. No headlights were permitted, only tiny "cat-eye" blackout lights on the front and rear of the truck that everyone called the "Jimmy." Each truck carried three cat eyes, two ruby-colored slits on the rear and a white slit on the right front grill that sparkled like a tiny jewel in the dark but was unseen from the air. Cat eyes were designed to identify a truck, not to illuminate its path.

The front bumper of Rookard's Jimmy disappeared into the channel, and seawater rose over the running boards to the bottom of the doors, spilled onto the floor of the cab, and sloshed around the engine crankcase. Rookard could feel his heart racing and the sweat beading on his forehead and spreading under his arms. It seemed like miles to the beach—he knew that if the truck stalled, he and Blackwell would have to swim to shore and there was no telling how far that was. There also was no telling who or what was out there.

Rookard was consoled that thousands of Americans had preceded him onto Utah Beach. A month before, infantrymen of the U.S. Fourth Division had come ashore on D-Day, 6 June 1944, on this same beach. He was also reassured that other trucks in his company were following, their drivers keyed on the ruby cat eyes of the trucks in front of them as they drove off the Navy landing craft. Rookard silently urged his Jimmy on as though it were a horse in need of coaxing. The vehicle had been adapted to make it to shore. Rookard and his comrades had prepared for the drive into the surf by waterproofing critical engine parts and fashioning air hoses that were clamped to the truck body so that carburetors and exhaust pipes could breathe.

Rookard's Jimmy inched forward on the seafloor and reached dry land. Dark images of Americans troops, moving about on the beach, suddenly appeared, and faceless military police, identified by the white letters "MP" on the faces of their helmets, waved Rookard forward to a narrow road leading inland. He was startled by sudden flashes lighting the horizon and followed, moments later, by rumblings that reminded him of an approaching thunderstorm. The bursts of light came from American and German artillery that boomed at each other. Close by, streaks of red and white light arched and twisted skyward in ghostly silence as though spewed from some supernatural and mysterious source. Rookard knew from months of training that these were tracer bullets used to guide machine gunners to the target. At night, they appeared to weave in the sky and play games of tag before vanishing like meteors. Rookard and Blackwell had never seen white tracers before, but they knew what they were and what they meant. Somewhere beyond this darkened road, Germans were firing these searing, glowing bullets, and the two Americans knew that the front was not far away.[1]

C Company, of the all-black 514th Quartermaster Truck Regiment, was landing on the shores of France. The wait was over. Like the rest of his comrades, Rookard was frightened—and with reason. The loads that he and his comrades were carrying contained ammunition and jerricans filled with gasoline stacked high in the cargo beds. The trucks were motorized bombs waiting for a spark.

The fighting had moved inland by the time C Company landed at Utah Beach, but the war was not far distant. The Germans contained the Allies in a narrow bridgehead extending only 20 miles at its greatest depth, and, in some places, the front was as close as 5 miles. The shelling of the beaches had all but ceased except for a sporadic round or two, and the Luftwaffe in France had been virtually destroyed. What was left of it dared to come out only occasionally at night. But the sounds and sights of war in the Normandy bridgehead were all around, and another three weeks would pass before the Allies broke out.

C Company wasn't the only unit of the 514th Regiment landing in Normandy in early July. I Company came ashore at Omaha where the beach extends several hundred yards inland before turning into bluffs that rise a hundred feet or more to overlook the water. It was here that the Germans had poured down fire on the men of the 1st and 29th Divisions as they had struggled ashore at dawn on 6 June. By day's end, more than two thousand Americans had died on the beaches of Normandy.

I Company had sailed from Southampton, England, to France with its trucks on a ship that weaved through the hundreds of vessels coming and going from the invasion beaches. Cpl. Edwin L. Brice, a member of I Company and the unit's historian, sketched in words the vast canvas of war witnessed by his comrades as the ship departed Southampton harbor:

> Far out on the horizon we could see the outlines of the gray battleships of the allied fleets, that were our protection. The next day we dropped anchor in the Bay of the Seine, in the artificial harbor that had been constructed by our engineers. . . . Here we were in a veritable forest of ships. The vessels moved in towards shore, through a maze of wrecked hulls, which stood out of the water all around us, with a caution that was breathtaking. . . . Before us, getting larger and larger were segments of the fabulous Atlantic Wall, as our vessel edged toward shore.
>
> Ashore could be seen vehicles winding back and forth up a road cut in the side of the cliff. C-47s were landing and taking off behind the brow of the cliff like subway trains in Times Square during rush hour. Seabees, who seemed to take their hazardous occupation as a matter of course, landed us and our trucks on the beach.[2]

For months, these men of C and I Companies, the 3903d and the 3909th Quartermaster (QM) Truck Companies, respectively, and the other ten companies of the 514th, had been objects of considerable derision, as were all Transportation Corps troops. They were perceived as noncombatants who had the cushy job of transporting supplies back and forth in the security of rear areas far from the front lines.

Generally, this had been their experience in past wars. In World War I, for example, although trucks did occasionally come under artillery fire, supply troops seldom saw action against the enemy. The growing numbers of trucks used in that conflict carried supplies to the forward areas and then retired.

But things had changed. Given time to develop in the years since World War I, the truck had dramatically altered warfare, mechanized it, and made it possible for armies to advance scores of miles each day and to outflank enemy positions with far greater speed than ever before. American Army generals in France quickly learned that trucks and drivers were often exposed to enemy fire, and, in this new, highly mobile warfare that developed in France, truckers often found themselves in combat.

Just three weeks before, on D-Day, when a number of trucking companies had landed in these same waters in the later waves at Omaha Beach, the men were shelled, shot at, and strafed while they struggled to drive their trucks through the surf and onto the beaches. When the ramp went down on one landing craft, drivers from the 3683d QM Truck Company found themselves bracketed by shells from German 88-mm guns as they pressed on to shore. The din of battle was deafening, and geysers erupting from the explosions sent columns of seawater splashing over the Jimmies. Some trucks stalled or were destroyed in the surf and were either abandoned or pulled to shore by bulldozers.

Once on land, there was no respite from the fire. Despite the intensity of the fighting and their exposure to the enemy, the drivers were immediately ordered to haul their cargoes of ammunition to the beleaguered American infantrymen struggling to push the Germans back from the beaches.

One private landed at two-thirty on D-Day and dodged bombs and shells as he hauled ammunition forward. The fighting was just as fierce the next day when his assistant driver was shot through the head as they neared the front.[3]

When the truckers returned to the expanding beach depots to reload, shells from German 88-mm guns and bullets continued to rain down. "Eighty-eight's were hitting all around us," another driver said. "Every time I'd start to drive I dove for a ditch or a slit trench." Trucks stalled in shell holes, and bombs ripped open radiators, riddled tires, and set gas tanks ablaze.[4]

A QM trucker surprised himself by shooting down a German fighter skimming over the beach area. The driver had jumped into the machine-gun ring above the truck cab and opened fire as the plane streaked by.[5]

A history of the Transportation Corps' Motor Transport Brigade (MTB), which had overall command of many of the trucking companies in the ETO and later organized and operated the Red Ball Express, recorded the struggles of the drivers and noted tersely that this war "destroyed the myth that trucking is rear echelon work."[6]

But the men in the majority of the trucking units faced problems far beyond those of being branded noncombatant truck drivers. They were black and encountered never-ending contempt in the military because of the color of their skin.

Although some trucking units consisted of all whites, about 70 percent of the transportation companies were manned by African Americans because most blacks were relegated to service units. It had been the Army's attitude for years, dating back to the eighteenth century, that blacks lacked the intellectual capacity and the fortitude to fight in integrated combat units. Yet, young black men had the same pride and dreams of glory as white men. They knew that they were good enough, given the chance and the respect, to fight shoulder to shoulder with whites. When he went to war, Rookard had dreamed of being one of the legendary Buffalo Soldiers of the western frontier. But that dream had died in the white man's army.

Of course, African Americans did more than drive trucks. They manned engineer units that kept open the supply routes, they served in ordnance companies that maintained trucks and depots, and they comprised 77 percent of the soldier-stevedores in port battalions who unloaded the ships bringing in supplies to the ETO from Britain and America.

Blacks also served in a few segregated combat units. The largest of these were the 92d Infantry Division, which fought in Italy, and the 93d Infantry Division, which served in the South Pacific. The most famous of the black combat units was the 332d Fighter Group, better known as the "Tuskegee Airmen," which consisted of the 99th, 100th, 301st, and 302d Fighter Squadrons.

Blacks were also mobilized into segregated artillery and armored units. Several all-black artillery battalions served in the ETO. The 761st Tank Battalion distinguished itself in 183 days of combat in Europe. The 761st was one of three black tank battalions that also included the 784th and the 827th.

At the very end of the war, a few blacks were integrated into white combat units but only by platoon and not by individual. In February 1945, three months before V-E Day, May 6, the day Germany surrendered, 2,200 black infantrymen were assigned to several all-white infantry divisions advancing into Germany. They served in these units with distinction, and many of their white officers and sergeants were astonished by the courage and determination of these black warriors.[7]

Men such as Rookard and Blackwell learned from their war experiences that whites seldom acknowledged the significant contributions of black truck drivers and service troops to the war in Europe. By V-E Day, black drivers were responsible for much of the 22,644,609 tons of supplies that had been transported to the front on the Red Ball Express and the other express trucking lines in the ETO.

"We never got enough credit for what we did," former Platoon Sgt. John Houston said. Fifty years after serving with C Company, much of it on the Red Ball Express, Houston managed the career of his daughter, singer and actress Whitney Houston. "I always felt the Army would never have won without us. We lugged an awful lot of stuff to the front, particularly to Third Army."[8]

On the July night that C Company came ashore in Normandy, Rookard and Blackwell groped forward in the blackness beyond the beach. As the company moved forward, each man dealt with fear in his own way. "I was scared," Rookard said. "We couldn't see a damned thing so we just drove on and kept moving until the company assembled." Luck favored both I and C Companies. They made it into Normandy without casualties.[9]

C Company bivouacked in the dark near the village of Sainte-Mère-Église. It was here, in the predawn darkness of D-Day, that troops of the 101st Airborne Division had accidentally parachuted into the center of the village where German soldiers were gathered to help douse a house fire. Many of the paratroopers were shot and killed as they floated down.

Sainte-Mère-Église was far enough away from the front lines when C Company arrived that there was little chance of attack from ground or air. Even so, it was wise to be vigilant. The Germans were in the habit of sending an occasional fighter flying over the bridgehead on a nighttime strafing run, and the enemy planes came and went so fast it was difficult to shoot them down. Veterans of the Normandy campaign were entertained by Bed Check Charlie, the lone German raider who flew low over the bridgehead nightly and shot at them as he passed by. Damage was minimal, and Bed Check seems to have been more of a diversion from boredom than an object of fear. He set an occasional supply dump ablaze. The greatest danger, however, came not from Bed Check's guns but from allied antiaircraft shells. Every ack-ack gun around opened up as the Americans fired at the streaking German. The plane usually escaped, but shrapnel from exploding shells rained down on the ground troops. Many soldiers in the rear wore helmets or slept under trucks to protect themselves from the falling debris of shells aimed at Bed Check.

The aftermath of the carnage at Sainte-Mère-Église was evident to the men of C Company when the sun rose the next day, but Sgt. James Bailey immediately assembled the scattered trucks and drivers and prepared his platoon for the road. The first order of business was to remove the waterproofing on each vehicle. In maintenance areas set up for that purpose, the men stripped the trucks of the coating that protected wires and plugs. They checked batteries, reopened distributor vents, checked engine oil for water, and removed air hoses.

Each truck retained the small sticker pasted on the lower left side of the windshield. On the inside, facing the driver, were instructions for all personnel landing at Normandy. "Just Before You Wade," it began. Then came the checklist of ten items. The outside of the sticker was a small red, white, and blue emblem of the American flag designed to identify the trucks in the Normandy battle zone.

C Company trucks were immediately ordered back to the beaches to pick up and deliver supplies to forward depots. The stiff German resistance had confined the supply dumps, as it had the troops, and depots were spotted everywhere in the Allied area of Normandy. Depots for gasoline, ammunition, rations, weapons, and clothing were located in fields and along the sides of roads, some close enough to the enemy that there was always danger to the truckers of running into German lines. Some drivers were issued fragmentation grenades to destroy their own trucks and cargoes if their vehicles broke down near the front. When one truck stalled within rifle shot of the Germans, the driver and his assistant slapped a grenade on the side of the truck before beating a hasty retreat, but the explosive failed to detonate. The driver returned the next day to find his vehicle undisturbed.[10]

"We were assigned where we were needed. There was no schedule because there was no schedule," Blackwell said. The men rose early, showered, shaved, ate breakfast, and then waited for orders. As requests for supplies filtered in, trucks were assigned to jobs individually or by platoon. "When our section sergeant told us where to go, that's where we went," Rookard added. "First platoon might go one way while second and third platoon went another."[11]

When Brice awoke the next morning, he was startled by the aftermath of war around the company's encampment near Omaha Beach. Brice recorded his observations:

> The surrounding shells of masonry that once were buildings, wrecked gun emplacements, beached and fire gutted LSM (Landing Ship Medium) and LSTs (Landing Ship Tank), shell craters, and machine gun scarred walls, all gave mute evidence of the terrific struggle that ensued here. . . . Overturned and charred remains of vehicles line the road, unexploded ammunition may be seen by merely looking down at any point. Fire scorched and disabled tanks with traction surfaces facing the sky and turrets in roadside ditches come into view. We pass a German plane lying in a nearby field. . . . Mixed with it all is to be seen a great profusion of enemy personal gear.[12]

As I Company trucks began to roll with supplies, the drivers were warned about mines along the shoulders and about shell fire because much of the road network was within range of German artillery. Corporal Brice wrote:

> Roadsigns reading "Road and Shoulders Clear of Mines" or "Mines Cleared to Hedges" flashed by at regular intervals. On the outskirts of St. Sauveur-le-Vicomte, our passage over an engineer constructed bridge is regulated by a large red lettered sign reading, "One Vehicle Over Bridge at a Time. Bridge Under Fire." Vehicles toward the end of our convoy narrowly missed being hit as shells were dropped on the bank adjacent to the bridge structure.[13]

The roads in the bridgehead were clogged with trucks, and traffic jams were common, particularly in the battered towns and villages of the Cotentin Peninsula. Ernie Pyle complained about the difficulties of getting around when he described how a huge M-19 tow truck, known as a "Prime Mover," clogged traffic for miles as it moved slowly along a road too narrow for other vehicles to pass.[14]

Transportation Corps trucks also got tangled with trucks and other vehicles from infantry divisions, antiaircraft batteries, engineering outfits, or any of the hundreds of units that crowded the roads in the bridgehead. By 1 July, three weeks after D-Day, upward of 71,000 vehicles, a large percentage of them trucks, had been landed for the American Army over Utah and Omaha Beaches, and they were pouring into France at a rate of about 3,000 a day. D-Day planners had expected to have nearly 110,000 vehicles ashore by the end of June, but the violent storm that swept through the channel in mid-June had disrupted the unloading process.[15]

The Army funneled traffic onto the Valognes-Bayeux highway, the main coastal route in Normandy that stretched to Cherbourg and the only good paved road on the beachhead until mid-July. More than 1,000 vehicles an hour passed through the four intersections on this thoroughfare between Omaha and Utah Beaches. At another junction point on the road from the beaches to the Saint-Lô area, a traffic count recorded 1,700 vehicles per hour.[16]

Most of the roads in the bridgehead had not been built for such heavy vehicles, and the Army discovered that the secondary roads in Normandy were disintegrating under the constant traffic. The Americans and Germans also had shelled and bombed the highways and byways of the Cotentin Peninsula from Cherbourg to Saint-Lô and later south of Saint-Lô around Avranches, which made them even more difficult to navigate. A member of an ordnance company was surprised by the "holes of many dimensions," the "tremendous cracks and huge chunks of asphalt that were savagely ripped out of place."[17]

Army engineer units were responsible for repairing the roadways of Normandy, and they worked nonstop to keep the highway network open throughout July. They filled shell holes and bomb craters and repaired damage inflicted by heavy vehicles and traffic. Road repair operations became more frantic as the fighting intensified in late July and during August.

Sgt. Henry E. Giles, with the 291st Engineer Combat Battalion, experienced the strain of maintaining the roads for the onrushing combat formations:

> This has been one of the meanest stretches of roadwork we've had. The traffic is heavy & the dust fogs up & we're hot & sweaty & it settles on us & turns to mud. The worst thing, is the stink. The hot weather soon bloats all the dead cows & horses & there must be a million of them. . . . The campaign in Northern France will be recalled for innumerable dead cows and horses in the first half of the campaign. . . . Nothing (thank heaven) can compare with the smell of a deceased horse or cow. Above all it is extremely difficult to bury an animal in that condition—so much digging is required.[18]

The stalemate in the bridgehead in June and through most of July deeply concerned the Allied high command. The generals feared that the western front in World War II would become static trench warfare similar to that of World War I. Even without airpower, the German Seventh Army was formidable and seasoned, and it gave ground sparingly. Most of the American infantry had never been in battle. The experience was new and frightening to the Americans, whereas many of the German troops were combat tested and knew their way around a battlefield.

For the Allies, the situation was becoming serious. They needed maneuvering room to take advantage of their strengths of a vastly superior air force, numerically superior tank forces, endless supplies of munitions and gasoline, and manpower reserves that would eventually overwhelm the Germans.

The break for the Allies came on 25 July with Operation Cobra.

TWO

OPERATION COBRA

On 25 July 1944, dawn tinted the horizon, imperceptibly at first, then the black, dimensionless landscape of Normandy reappeared from beneath a nocturnal mantle to reveal a light green patchwork of fields and high hedges. The silence at first light was occasionally shattered by the dry, brittle rattle of German machine guns lashing out over deserted pastures and answered by the rhythmic cracking of American semiautomatic M-1s.

Along a line that extended across the base of the Cotentin Peninsula, several hundred thousand men from the German Seventh Army and the American First Army were poised opposite each other in the increasingly desperate struggle for northern France. As the sun climbed from the east, the sounds of war again would rise to a deafening crescendo in Normandy as the Americans fought to dislodge the enemy.

It had been seven weeks since the D-Day invasion and the vaunted German Army's grip on the Normandy bridgehead seemed unbreakable. To the east at Caen, the Germans had checked Gen. Sir Bernard Montgomery's army of British and Canadians. To the west, the Americans had captured the Cotentin Peninsula, but progress was slow through the *bocage* (hedgerow country) with its boggy pastures surrounded by centuries-old hedges. The fighting in each enclosed field was a war unto itself that stymied the Americans and consumed men and machines. The nature of the battlefront aided the Germans. The enemy placed machine guns in the thick hedges at one end of a field, and the Americans had to rout the gunners who always fell back to similar preprepared positions in adjacent fields. The Allies had already suffered 122,000 casualties, staggering losses for so little captured ground. Desperate measures were needed for a breakthrough.[1]

Lt. Gen. Omar N. Bradley, commander of the American First Army, believed that he had a strategy to force a breakout. The day of 25 July would begin as any other day along the American front, which stretched from Lessay, on the Gulf of Saint-Malo, some 50 miles eastward to the Caumont area, where it met Montgomery's 21st Army Group. Bradley wanted the Germans to believe that dawn would bring more of the same intense fighting as the Americans sought to push the Germans back.

But, on the 25th, the quiet at sunrise strangely lingered in a 10-mile area just west of Saint-Lô. The Americans were unnaturally inactive. Soon after dawn, reports began filtering into German Army headquarters that the Americans were abandoning their positions. "Looks as if they've got cold feet," chortled Kurt Kauffmann, operations officer for the Panzer Lehr Division.[2]

The Germans had other reasons to relax besides a lessening of the American pressure and a sense of superiority at witnessing the flight of these green, untested "amis," as the Germans nicknamed the Americans. The weather had cleared, and the sun was shining. For weeks, the armies had fought in a cold, damp climate, in which the sun seldom appeared and rains made the fields soggy and impassable.

From the north, however, the German Seventh faced an unimaginable storm sweeping in over the channel. It began around nine o'clock in the morning with distant rumbling. A half hour later, the German lines within a 10-mile box near Saint-Lô were swept by a cataclysmic typhoon that rolled over them for more than two hours. When the storm finally subsided, it left a swath of moonscape that once had been German foxholes, fortifications, and front line. The German grip on Normandy was about to be broken.

Bradley's bold plan, code-named Cobra, employed nearly two thousand planes of the U.S. Eighth and Ninth Air Forces, many of them B-24 and B-17 heavy bombers. On the morning of the 25th, the skies above England throbbed as the planes formed up for the short flight to France. Flying in waves at 12,000 feet, they carried high-explosive bombs and orders to unload them in the Saint-Lô sector by using the Saint-Lô–Periers Road as the targeting point.

"They came with a terrible slowness," Ernie Pyle wrote. He continued:

> "They came in flights of twelve, three flights to a group and in groups stretched out across the sky. They came in "families" of about seventy planes each.
>
> The flight across the sky was slow and studied. I've never known a storm or a machine, or any resolve of man that had about it the aura of such a ghastly relentlessness. I had the feeling that even had God appeared beseechingly before them in the sky, with palms outstretched to persuade them back, they would not have had within them the power to turn their irresistible course.[3]

"The planes kept coming overhead like a conveyor belt," recalled Generalmajor Fritz Bayerlein, commander of Panzer Lehr, which was among the best armored divisions in the German Army. "The bomb carpets came down, now ahead, now on the right, now on the left. . . . The fields were burning and smoldering. . . . My front lines looked like a landscape on the moon, and at least seventy percent of my personnel were out of action—dead, wounded, crazed or numb.[4]

There was no respite from the bombs. Even Americans were caught in the maelstrom. Pyle wrote:

> Many times I've heard bombs whistle or swish or rustle, but never before had I heard bombs rattle. I still don't know the explanation of it. But it was an awful sound. I remember hitting the

ground flat all spread out like the cartoons of people flattened by steam rollers, and then squirming like an eel to get under one of the heavy wagons in the shed.

There is no description of the sound and fury of those bombs except to say it was chaos, and a waiting for darkness. The feeling of the blast was sensational. The air struck us in hundreds of continuing flutters. Our ears drummed and rang.[5]

A total of 111 American troops were killed and 490 wounded by "shorts"—bombs that fell in American-held areas when dust from the bombardment obscured the target area and blew back over American lines.[6] The incoming waves of bombers targeted the billowing dust cloud rather than the German line. Among the dead was Lt. Gen. Leslie McNair, commanding general of the U.S. Continental Training Command, who was visiting the front that day. The only way that graves registration troops could identify McNair was by the three-star lapel pin found on a mangled, unrecognizable corpse. McNair was the highest-ranking American officer killed during World War II.[7]

When the planes had left, American infantry troops tentatively moved through the devastation. They expected the same deadly, slow progress of the past month, but as Sherman tanks from Maj. Gen. J. Lawton Collins's VII Corps began to roll through the target area, the pace picked up. Except for isolated outposts and occasional undaunted German soldiers, the enemy had nothing left with which to stop the Americans. Bradley had accomplished his breakout, and one of the greatest routs in military history was about to begin.

Two days after the bombardment, the Americans had punched a bulge in the German lines in front of Saint-Lô nearly 15 miles wide and 10 miles deep. By 31 July, the American line was swinging eastward toward Paris like a giant gate, hinged at Caumont where it met the British, and sweeping the German Seventh Army from its path. On 1 August, Lt. Gen. George S. Patton took command of the newly activated U.S. Third Army, and his armored columns rolled south and east out of Normandy.

Ernest Hemingway described the pursuit in one of his dispatches to the homefront: "The armies came out of the hedgerow country to the hills, then down into the plain; through pockets of German resistance and through towns that were ruined and untouched." The fighting "merged into a great blur of tiredness and dust, of the smell of earth new-broken by TNT, the grinding sound of tanks and bulldozers, the sound of automatic-rifle and machine-pistol fire, dry as a rattler rattling; and the quick spurting tap of the German light machine guns—and always waiting for others to come up."[8]

Patton's original mission was to employ the Third Army to clear Brittany of the German Army and capture the Breton ports so that supplies could flow through them to the American forces. With the collapse of the German Seventh Army, however, General Eisenhower ordered most of the Third Army eastward toward Paris, while Patton's Eighth Corps remained in Brittany to mop up the Germans and take the ports.

By 13 August, an American spearhead reached Le Mans, some 90 miles from Paris. The Allied armies captured Paris on 25 August, and the Americans swung south of the capital to pause in front of Troyes. The Allies now formed a continuous line on the west bank of the Seine from just south of Paris to the English Channel. The German Army was collapsing, and the road to Berlin seemed wide open.

BREAKOUT AND PURSUIT

In western Europe during August 1944, trucks and drivers played a pivotal role in the war. Their debut in the mechanized warfare that was to characterize the fighting across France came during the Allies' chaotic efforts to haul supplies to the front during late July and August, and they became major players in the ETO with the creation of the Red Ball Express. Once the German line had been breached, truckborne American infantry and armor broke through the openings to display a penchant for mobile warfare that carried them to the frontiers of the Reich by early September.

Such blitzkrieg-like breakthroughs by the Americans were not out of character for the American Army. Eisenhower, for one, understood and had encouraged this capability. The Supreme Commander noted in *Crusade in Europe* that the American Army had "always featured mobility in the organization and equipment of its forces. Before the advent of the motor car our Army was proportionately stronger in cavalry than most other armies of the time."[1]

Best known for their mobility in the American Army prior to World War II were the "horse soldiers" who defended the western frontier in the late nineteenth century. But Gen. George Washington had relied on mobility to avoid confrontation with the British during the American Revolution to keep his weaker army alive. Gen. Robert E. Lee had used similar tactics with his

Confederate Army of Northern Virginia to counter the more powerful Union Army of the Potomac. Union Gen. William T. Sherman had adopted a war of movement to bring Confederate armies in the southeastern states to their knees during his march to the sea. In 1944, nearly a century had passed since the American Army had fought a prolonged land war, and its capabilities were unknown to friend and foe alike.

The British had little respect for the U.S. Army and considered it poorly led and disciplined. They remembered the debacle of Kasserine Pass in Tunisia in February 1943, when Field Marshal Erwin Rommel's Afrika Korps routed inexperienced and complacent U.S. forces in the first major defeat of an American army by the Germans in World War II. Even as the American Army came ashore after D-Day in the summer of 1944, most of its troops and units were still untested in battle, and the fighting in Normandy had given it scant opportunity to demonstrate its strengths.

But France would be different. Once out of the bridgehead, American tanks and mechanized infantry rampaged across France as they chased the hapless enemy and surprised both the British and the Germans by their lightning advance. No one expected the Americans to outdo the Germans in blitzkrieg tactics. Right behind the U.S. combat forces came the trucks, thousands of them. In some cases, the Jimmies went ahead of the infantry to supply the fast-moving Shermans, and more than one trucker caught in enemy territory had to fight his way back to safety. In early August, truckborne American troops moved southwest toward Coutances, south to Avranches, and southeast toward Vire. By 31 July, the German Seventh Army had been driven from the Cherbourg Peninsula. By 9 August, the Third Army's trucks and infantry were sweeping through Brittany in an effort to capture the all-important ports, while the rest of the Third moved south and west toward Paris.

The Germans realized that, unless they could stop the Americans, they would lose northern France west of the Seine and most likely be driven from the country altogether. During the first week of August, Führer Adolf Hitler ordered a counterattack at Mortain in a desperate attempt to split the two advancing American armies and to destroy each one separately.

"We must strike like lightning," Hitler told members of his armed forces high command (OKW) staff on 2 August. According to military historian John Keegan, Hitler continued:

> When we reach the sea the American spearheads will be cut off.
> . . . We might even be able to cut off their entire bridgehead. We
> must not get bogged down in cutting off the Americans who
> have broken through. Their turn will come later. We must
> wheel north like lightning and turn the entire enemy front from
> the rear.[2]

But the German attack failed. During the ensuing fight, the German Seventh Army and the newly designated Fifth Panzer Army were virtually destroyed. As the German formations drove forward to split the U.S. First Army, to the north, from the U.S. Third Army, to the south, they formed a salient between the two American armies and exposed themselves to encirclement by the Allies. Forces from Montgomery's 21st Army Group pushed south from Caen as American forces moved northward toward the town of Falaise to encircle the enemy. Some 200,000 Germans became prisoners, 50,000 Germans were killed, and much of their equipment was destroyed. The remnants of the German Seventh fled across the Seine toward Germany with the Americans close at their heels.[3]

It was uncharacteristic of a German army to break and flee, but the disintegration of the German forces had more to do with leadership deficiencies than with the fighting qualities of the German soldier. The enemy troops had conducted themselves well in containing the Normandy bridgehead for nearly two months without benefit of airpower.

Military historian Maj. Gen. J. C. F. Fuller claimed that the destruction of the German Seventh Army was Hitler's doing: "The mistake Hitler made was not so much to order the attack [at Mortain], as to refuse to allow von Kluge [the German commander] to withdraw once he was decisively checked." The delay in the withdrawal meant that the Seventh Army became trapped around Falaise.[4]

Although some 300,000 German troops escaped the Falaise pocket and retreated over the Seine, they were little more than a rabble incapable of a serious fight. They fled from the advancing American armored columns toward the fortifications along the German frontier and turned only occasionally to fight behind the rivers Marne, Moselle, Meuse, and Aisne, where they knew a few troops could delay their pursuers.

No one in the Allied high command had anticipated this rout. D-Day planners had predicted a slow, methodical Allied push eastward through northern and eastern France with the Germans fighting delaying actions as they withdrew. Eisenhower, in *Crusade in Europe,* wrote that the most logical strategy for Hitler in the defense of northern France would have been to swing his troops back from the Normandy area, make a stand along the Seine, and contest every crossing by the Americans and British. "If he [Hitler] had chosen to do this he could undoubtedly have made a stubborn defense of that obstacle [the Seine] until our advancing troops were able to outflank him and force evacuation."[5]

Operation Overlord (code name for the northwestern European invasion by the Allies) planners had expected the Americans to reach the Seine by D-Day plus 90—6 September—where the Allied armies were to halt while a depot system and supply base were developed. (The Allies actually reached the Seine by D-Day plus 79.) The depots were to be positioned in the area between Rennes, at the base of the Breton Peninsula, and the city of Laval, some 10 miles to the east, to create a supply base closer to American troops along the Seine, which could more easily support their needs when they advanced toward Germany. The West Wall fortifications protecting the Reich around Aachen were not expected to be reached by American forces until D-Day plus 330, or May 1945.[6]

This slow-moving strategy would have solved most of the Allies' logistical problems. Eisenhower noted that, if the Germans had fallen back slowly, "our lines of communication would have been relatively short and the logistic problem would have been solved gradually, conforming to the pace that our own troops could advance."[7]

But the German defeat at Falaise altered these plans. The battered and fleeing enemy was too enticing a quarry to allow it to retreat unchallenged to the West Wall. On 19 August, Eisenhower authorized Patton, Bradley, and Montgomery to cross the Seine in hot pursuit. The hope was that the German armies in France could be destroyed before reaching their homeland, despite fears that the advancing Americans would outrun their supplies. Eisenhower knew that this decision imposed a much greater burden on the Americans than on the British, whose supply lines were not as extended. According to historian Roland Ruppenthal, the pursuit created "a supply task out of all proportion to planned capabilities. . . . With the supply structure already severely strained by the speed with which the last 200 miles had been covered, these decisions entailed the risk of a complete breakdown."[8] Nevertheless, Eisenhower gave the order, and the race against time and supplies began.

Adding to the difficulties of supplying American forces was the fact that the Army was supporting more U.S. troops in France than had originally been anticipated. The Communication Zone (COMZ), the command responsible for lines of communication and logistics in the liberated areas, had expected supply responsibilities for twelve divisions in the first ninety days following the invasion and then only in the area west of the Seine. COMZ also did not expect to support and provision these forces in any offensive action beyond the river until after September 1944. Only in October did it plan to supply a "minor advance" beyond the Aisne River, about 75 miles east of the Seine.

By 4 September, however, COMZ was supporting sixteen, instead of twelve, U.S. divisions 150 miles beyond the Seine, and ten days later, First Army forces were operating at the German border in the vicinity of Aachen, well over 200 miles beyond Paris.[9] Overlord planners also had never envisioned Patton's Third Army slicing through Lorraine and becoming a large independent army that could threaten the German heartland. Patton's drive was to have been only a small, secondary effort south of the Ardennes, targeted at Verdun and Metz, to divert enemy resistance from the main allied thrust by the First Army in the north. A second objective of the Third was to link up with the U.S. 6th Army Group moving up the Rhône Valley after its landing near Saint-Tropez and prevent the escape of enemy troops from southwestern France into Germany. The 6th Army Group, commanded by Lt. Gen. Jacob Devers, had come ashore in Operation Dragoon on 15 August 1944.

Because of the rapidity and success of the American advance, the original Overlord plan was modified to allow Patton to launch a major drive south of the Ardennes into eastern France, even as the main allied effort was still to be made in the north.[10] But this meant that COMZ was now responsible for supplying a larger Third Army.

With the Germans in full retreat, the American Army was transformed, despite its logistical problems. What had formerly been a tentative force became a roaring menace that made full use of mechanization. Historian Lida Mayo wrote that this new mechanized force of almost unimaginable numbers included scores of thousands of trucks, jeeps, command cars, tanks, tank transporters, wreckers, and even refrigerator trucks that formed huge convoys, all heading out of Normandy. They carried everything imaginable to fight the war—troops, ammunition, gasoline, rations, telephone poles, boats for river crossings, and even mobile work and repair shops. Trucks and jeeps dragged artillery pieces to the front, and, occasionally, a general's mobile headquarters was hauled to a new location.[11]

Corporal Brice recorded I Company's moves during the pursuit:

> At any hour of the day or night, members of the truck company have to be prepared to be galvanized into action. Truck mainte-

.

nance must be constant so that trucks are ready to roll at any
hour. Such an hour struck at 2400 hours tonight. The midnight
air was rent with the cries of Lieutenant Harnist and dispatcher
Peay crying, "Everybody up. Get ready to roll at once. Let's go."
Soon the sound of motors being warmed up provided a purring
background to the staccato of sharp orders of officers and non-
coms. The call for all drivers to assemble for convoy instructions
signaled that preparations for movement had been completed.
The thin blackout slits of the trucks gave an eerie appearance to
the setting amid the apple trees in our Normandy orchard
bivouac area. The order "Wind 'em up" was given and slowly, at
measured intervals each truck rolled out into the night until the
whole convoy wound out of the area down the road and off into
the distance. Meanwhile, we, left back at headquarters, strain to
catch the last sound of the motors in the otherwise quiet night.
The ruby tail lights finally fade away over the distant crest and
they are gone.[12]

The mission of these I Company trucks was to carry ammunition from one advanced supply point (ASP) east of Saint-
Sauveur-le-Vicomte to ASP 803, located near the front. To Corporal Brice, it looked like a big push. "Ammunition is not even
unloaded at ASPs now, but kept on the trucks and moved still
further on with the advance."[13]

I and C Companies were helping to supply one of the swiftest
advances in the history of land warfare. Historian Martin Blumenson described the pursuit as resembling "a stampede of wild horses
. . . fast and fluid," almost without control. He added:

The dust that was kicked up did not obscure the fact that a mass
of allied movement east of the Seine took place, a gigantic and
sometimes haphazard closing action of all available forces
toward Germany in which a frantic search for a bridge still
intact was often the most significant detail.

Thinly spread, both laterally and in depth, the armies over-
ran and liberated northern France. . . . Reconnaissance units

and cavalry swept far and wide, clearing great areas, particularly on the flanks, to free infantry and armor for advance along the main highways. . . .

There was only sporadic contact with the enemy along the fronts of the onrushing armies. Only in a few instances did the Germans try to make a stand, usually at river-crossing sites. The inadequacy of the German forces, their lack of communications, their drastic shortages of equipment, and what seemed to be command confusion on the lower levels led to the abandonment of any pretense of reestablishing a line anywhere except at the West Wall. . . .

For the soldiers, the countryside had become a monotonous blur of changing scenery. Their eyes bloodshot and tear-filled from sun, wind, dust and weariness, they followed the blinding road all day long and at night strained to keep the cat eyes of the vehicle ahead in sight.[14]

By the end of August, troops of Montgomery's 21st Army Group were approaching Brussels and the port of Antwerp. Lt. Gen. Courtney Hodges's First Army was driving toward the Aachen area on the German frontier, and Patton's Third Army was besieging the city of Metz, less than 50 miles from the German frontier. (Hodges had taken command of the First Army when Bradley became army group commander.)

Patton, more than anyone, knew that the key to this advance was the trucks. Without them, his tanks and infantry could not have advanced. He paid tribute to his Jimmies in a lengthy press release titled "The 2½-ton Truck Is Our Most Valuable Weapon," which Corporal Brice quoted in his history:

The 2½ tons were seldom empty, never idle, throughout the Third Army's smashing drive. They hauled gasoline, rations, ammunition and fighting men forward, returned ever full with German prisoners, or wounded or dead Americans. Many times they were called upon to move infantry. Frequently, they carried the "doggies" [infantry] into the streets of towns held by the enemy, unloading them under fire. They carried anything, anywhere, anytime. That's all—but it merited for them the title "our most important weapon."[15]

"We are really operating in earnest now," Brice wrote in his history, as Patton's drive continued into August and September. "Rail lines are down, consequently, our trucks are in constant demand."[16]

FOUR

IN HARM'S WAY

American armor and infantry advanced so rapidly through northern France in August 1944 that it was impossible to establish a fixed system of supply depots near the front. Orders for supply vehicles to rendezvous at designated forward depots were meaningless when trucks arrived at their destinations. The depots were gone—moved on with the combat forces shifting forward every day, sometimes every hour.

"Sometimes ammunition convoys were diverted to points as much as twenty miles beyond their original destinations and when they arrived at a new area they would have to wait while it was cleared of enemy troops," historian Mayo wrote.[1]

The Army improvised to get critical supplies to the troops. Jimmies became rolling depots that followed the infantry. The VIII Corps converted massive tank transporters into rolling ASPs whose flatbed trailers carried loads of up to 50 tons of ammunition and loaded jerricans and followed the infantry and armor. Jimmies also began delivering right to the front lines or, more accurately, where the infantry and armor happened to be engaged in combat.

Lt. William A. Harnist led a platoon of I Company Jimmies on a mission to deliver "repple depples" (replacements) to the 4th Armored Division as it advanced across the Breton Peninsula toward Brest:

We went hightailing along through Rennes, right past the front line and [American] infantrymen who were still sitting in their foxholes. My men said, "Open it up, Lieutenant," and we did. We flew like hell. Our job was to follow armor and we caught up with Combat Command A (CCA) 50 miles ahead of the infantry.[2]

Sometimes, even the infantry and repple depples couldn't find the front. Before the 35th Division was trucked from Mortain to Le Mans, the division's destination was changed twice because of the constantly changing front, and the itinerary was changed three times before the vehicles departed. En route, traffic-directing military police (MPs) were constantly receiving new orders that broke the convoy into platoon-size units that lost contact with each other. As leading elements of the division reached the outskirts of Le Mans, the Germans had continued their retreat beyond the city.[3]

The Army relied heavily on the drivers and platoon commanders to bring order to the confusion of mechanized warfare. By the time the truckers of the 3630th QM Truck Company returned from their mission of transporting the 35th Division, they had driven 225 miles and had been at the wheel for 42 hours. Every truck had arrived at its assigned destination, and the entire division had been moved.

The main link that held the front and rear units together and prevented total confusion was a radio network established in England by Col. John B. Medaris, ordnance officer for the First Army. Although it had been little used while the Allies were held in check in Normandy, Medaris kept it active for training purposes. Historian Mayo observed:

Now it came into its own, saving hours, sometimes days, in the transmittal of requests and the delivery of critical supplies to far-flung combat units and performing invaluable services in many ways; for example, ammunition men on the march could be directed to establish new ASP's as far forward as possible. Above all, the radio net provided for firm control of all types of supplies. Medaris and his staff knew at all times what was on hand, where it was, and what was needed.[4]

The rapidly changing battlefield brought truckers face to face with the enemy as U.S. tanks and mobile infantry advanced beyond German lines and left pockets of Wehrmacht troops behind through which the trucks had to pass. One trucker told of a convoy traveling at night that was slowed by traffic-directing MPs. As the trucks approached the MPs, the drivers were confused by their uniforms—the MPs were German. The story might be apocryphal, but it has a ring of truth because of the fluid combat situation and because the Germans could travel only at night as the result of Allied mastery of the air.

Martin Blumenson noted in *Breakout and Pursuit* that this "was a period of confusion, when a jeep load of soldiers who had missed a turn in the road might capture a village, when an anti-aircraft battery or a few truck drivers might inadvertently take a hundred German prisoners."[5]

Historian Sarah M. Davis wrote in a Third Army history titled *Patton's Wheels*:

> QM trucks had to fight their way through enemy pockets many times in order to maintain contact with the armored spearheads until the infantry had completed their mopping up operations. On some occasions enemy fire was so intense the truckers needed armored escort to bring their valuable cargoes through the forward elements.[6]

One twenty-truck convoy entered a French village believed to be in American hands and unexpectedly came under enemy small-arms fire. The driver and assistant driver of the lead Jimmy were forced to retreat on foot and returned fire as they dashed for safety. The driver made it back to American lines, but the assistant driver was killed.[7]

I Company's Cpl. Clifton Lucas reported his experiences on the mission to Brest:

> We were driving along the road and all at once we heard a great deal of firing. Directly ahead we saw a tank on fire and we all jumped out of the trucks and took cover. The major in charge of the replacements went up ahead to see what was happening and found that the Germans were firing on our convoy. We all took positions to return the fire. Some Germans were killed and others captured. We were finally forced to disperse the trucks in surrounding fields and unload the replacements. We stayed in the field all that night and took twelve prisoners. The next day about ten in the morning all hell cut loose. German eighty-eights started firing on us and on the trucks. Several trucks loaded with gasoline were hit and started burning fiercely. Tanks from the Sixth Division finally succeeded in silencing the eighty-eights.[8]

Brig. Gen. Charles Lanham, then a colonel commanding the 22d Infantry, 4th Division, praised the gallantry of bands of truckers during the pursuit as they enthusiastically engaged the enemy in combat:

> As daylight neared, confusion mounted. Our columns clogged in endless traffic jams, bogged down in bomb craters, crawled through detours over broken fields, struggled across improvised stream crossings. All around us the night erupted with flaming towns. German artillery and bombs added to the confusion. Every once in a while a huge German tank would pound out of the darkness and cut into our column, thinking it his. Running fights ebbed and flowed around us. As daylight broke, we were literally cheek by jowl with the Germans—in the same villages, in the same fields, in the same hedgerows, in the same farm yards. A hundred sporadic fights broke out—to the front, to the flanks, to the rear, within the columns, everywhere. It was early that morning that I first became aware of the fact that our

IN HARM'S WAY ■ 33

Negro truck drivers were leaving their trucks and whooping it up after German soldiers all over the landscape. This, I might add, is not hearsay. I personally saw it over and over again in the early hours of that wild morning. But in addition to my own personal observation, many reports reached me throughout the day of the voluntary participation of these troops in battle and their gallant conduct.[9]

Truck units were particularly vulnerable to air attacks, and the Luftwaffe put on a maximum effort to protect its beleaguered troops during the pursuit. Corporal Brice reported one air attack in Normandy:

The company made its first move last night to an area seven miles west of Granville. . . . On our first night in Bricquebec, we bivouacked in a wheat field. Everybody got busy digging slit trenches to sleep in. At dusk enemy aircraft began to roam the skies. There seemed to be all types of planes overhead. They droned up and down and set up a din that was ominous. Ninety's [90-mm antiaircraft guns] in nearby fields rent the air with protests. Now and then a fighter would come in low and the rat a tat of its machine guns would make us flinch inside our holes. Before long they set a nearby wheat field afire with flares or incendiaries. Our area guards put it out in short order and thus prevented it from spreading. Very late in the night the anti-aircraft gunners bagged a plane and it crashed streaming flame some distance away. Tracers were going up in streams all night giving the black moonless sky an appearance of a ghostly carnival. This was indeed a spectacular and marrow chilling night.

At nightfall [the next day] we bivouacked in a field south of Granville and Avranches but near a road that led to the famous abbey of Mont-Saint-Michel. The Abbey itself could be seen in the distance like a purple-gray pyramid. That night "Jerry" roared again overhead, and turned night into day with his flares. Guns barked all around us. The bridge and focal road junction at Avranches as well as an ASP near us seemed to be their goals.[10]

The 3398th QM Truck Company was attacked for several days in the same vicinity by German planes as its trucks carried supplies to Patton's army. The attacks began in the dark, just before dawn, as the Luftwaffe targeted the bridge near Avranches over which the 3398th was traveling. The planes dropped flares and then strafed and bombed the bridge and any trucks in its vicinity.

The attacks continued throughout the next day as the German fighters followed the convoy to its bivouac area. The truckers fought back and reported several planes shot down. Luck was with the company. Only one man was wounded and materiel damage was held to a minimum.[11]

The fighting in Normandy and Brittany left many of the towns and villages in shambles. Former Sgt. John Houston will never forget the devastation in such towns as Saint-Lô, Vire, La Haye du Puit, Coutances, and Avranches. In the words of historian Mayo, the Americans found "each town an awful monument to hell itself. The stench of unburied bodies lying in the unmerciful summer sun was overpowering at times, as the convoy rolled slowly on through the red clay dust which clung savagely to the skin and blinded the eyes."[12]

Snipers were always a serious threat, particularly when units moved forward to new bivouac areas as the Germans retreated. Journalist Ernie Pyle, who followed the pursuit, reported:

> The Germans have gone in for sniping in a wholesale manner. There are snipers everywhere. There are snipers in trees, in buildings, in piles of wreckage, in the grass. . . . Every mile we advance there are dozens of snipers left behind us. They pick off our soldiers one by one as they walk down the roads or across the fields. It isn't safe to move into a new bivouac area until the snipers have been cleaned out. The first bivouac I moved into had shots ringing through it for a full day before all the hidden

gunmen were rounded up. It gives you the same spooky feeling that you get on moving into a place you suspect of being sown with mines.[13]

But some encounters with the enemy offered comic relief for the weary soldiers. Corporal Brice noted one such incident after I Company made a move to a new bivouac area three miles south of Brou on N-155. The men settled in for another night fearful of mines, snipers, and even groups of German stragglers:

After erecting my pup tent I retired early. . . . It was dark as pitch and the deep woods of our area and the thick vegetation made the darkness seem all enveloping. About midnight, I heard [Don] Blandford [on guard duty] sing out, "Halt." Three shots rang out in quick succession followed by running feet, then more shots. I debated whether to go out and see what was going on and risk being shot by either side in the darkness, or staying where I was—alert. Soon I heard Lieutenant Stevens calling Blandford; and after a while heard him answer. I thought surely the boys were right this time and we had stumbled into a pocket of Germans. It was all right for the front to move fast, but these "Jerries" they left behind certainly made it tough for us supposedly non-combat troops.

In the morning Blandford's version of what had happened substantiated my fears and those of a great many others. He said a large body had crawled toward him in the darkness and ignored all of his orders to stop until he fired. Then only did it turn and run through the bushes.

[But, in the morning, Brice unmasked the "enemy".] This morning [21 August] First Sergeant Grant, Technician Fifth George Woods, Private First Class Harlan Childress and I were leaving the area en route to the ration depot, when a very large rabbit leisurely bounded across the field before our vehicle, without seeming in the least frightened of us or hurried. We looked at each other and saw that we were all, coincidentally, in agreement, that we had unquestionably discovered Blandford's intruder of the night before.[14]

Truckers were fiercely proud of their combat role. Brice noted:

Practically all the drivers point proudly to bullet holes in the cabs or windshields of their vehicles, acquired during the nightly runs through the avenue of snipers between their beach and the armor a few miles away. They speak of "the first guy who makes a crack about the QM being a soft life," rather belligerently.[15]

The company chaplain felt compelled to praise the truckers for their fighting spirit:

During Chaplain Gibson's address Sunday he told of a friend who smiled when he told him he was connected with a truck outfit. He also told us that he would know what to say to this friend the next time he met him, for trucks go right to the front lines in this war. . . . Without the superb endurance, heroism at times, and bravery of truckmen in completing their missions, along the lifelines to the front, under fire on many occasions, the rapid advances we have just made and are still making could not be accomplished.[16]

THE PORTS

The Red Ball Express was a child of necessity. Its birth resulted from the needs of the victorious American Army and Hitler's command to his troops to hold and destroy the French ports. Long before D-Day, Allied commanders had recognized that victory in the European Theater would depend on logistics. No matter how well their armies were trained or how well they fought, the troops had to be well supplied before they could take on the experienced German Army.

It was also understood that the key to supplying the armies in the ETO lay in the capture of the French ports in Brittany, Normandy, and along the coast of the English Channel from Normandy to the Belgian border. Once these ports were wrested from the Germans, the Allies could provide an unending stream of supplies and equipment to support the advancing armies. But capturing the ports would require time and intense fighting.

The invasion beaches were expected to serve as the main entry points onto the continent for both men and materiel for only about a month. By D-Day plus 30, Allied planners expected the port of Cherbourg at the tip of the Cotentin Peninsula, along with five smaller ports in Normandy, to be in American hands. By D-Day plus 60, the ports of Brest, Lorient, and Saint-Malo; Quiberon Bay; and other ports in Brittany were to have been captured from the enemy. Once all these ports were open, principally the Breton ports, they would serve as disembarkation points for men and supplies, and the invasion beaches would be phased out of operation.

According to Ruppenthal, the beaches and the Normandy ports, including Cherbourg, were expected to have a discharge capacity of about 27,000 long tons per day, enough to support twelve divisions on the continent. Once the Breton ports were in operation, after D-Day plus 60, the total discharge capacity on the continent was expected to rise to around 37,000 tons daily to support sixteen U.S. divisions. By D-Day plus 90, the total discharge capacity of all ports and beaches was expected to reach 46,000 tons daily, enough to supply the needs of twenty-one divisions fighting in France.[1]

Once the allies landed on June 6, however, the preliminary plans were of little value. Although the smaller Normandy ports were captured soon after the D-Day landings and Cherbourg fell on 27 June, it wasn't until the end of July that supplies in significant amounts were flowing through Cherbourg, the largest of the Normandy ports. The Germans had destroyed its harbor with Teutonic thoroughness.[2]

The minor Normandy ports of Isigny, Grandchamps-Maisy, Barfleur, Saint-Vaast-la-Hougue, and Carentan were of limited value in the massive and free-wheeling land war in northern France. As tidal ports, they were operational only at certain times of the day and were unable to handle deep-draft ships. Carentan was landlocked at the end of a 10-mile channel, and Isigny was also several miles inland. The average daily discharge from these ports was less than 1,000 tons except for Saint-Vaast, at which the average daily discharge was 1,172 tons.

The Breton ports were the prizes sought by the Americans. Preinvasion plans called for the Third Army to swing west into Brittany shortly after the invasion to clear the peninsula and capture Brest. Brest and Quiberon Bay were considered by Overlord planners to be of the greatest value to U.S. ground forces during the Allies' first six months in France. According to Ruppenthal, Quiberon Bay offered "a better solution to the problem [of port discharge] than did any other location on the northwest coast of France."[3] Troops and supplies would flow into these Breton ports and be transported directly to the front, which was expected to remain on the west bank of the Seine until October. Quiberon Bay had great potential as a port area with more than 3,000 yards of hard beach "of required slope" and a sheltered anchorage capable of accommodating some two hundred ships. Nearby were four minor ports that were suitable for "high-line discharge at first and for deep-water piers later."[4]

But the Germans refused to be accommodating. Although they were quickly driven from most of Brittany in early August, pockets of fanatical enemy troops held the Breton ports, as well as those along the channel coast, and stubbornly refused to surrender. German troops held Brest, Lorient, and Saint-Malo long after the Allies expected them to fall. The German garrison at Saint-Malo capitulated on 2 September, but Brest held out against the Allied siege until 18 September.

The Americans were able to develop several areas along the north shore of Brittany to offload supplies for troops clearing the peninsula. They included Morlaix, Saint-Michel en Greve, Saint-Brieuc, and Saint-Malo, but the tonnage capacity of these small ports was insignificant.[5]

With the breakout and unexpected speed and scope of the pursuit, however, the fighting for the Breton ports became a sideshow to events unfolding in northern and eastern France. It soon became apparent that these ports were no longer so valuable to the Americans.

Hitler had conceived the idea to hold and demolish the ports as part of his strategic plan to defeat the Allies or, at least, slow their advance by depriving the Americans of their advantage of abundant supplies. Declaring that all ports were to be fortresses, he assigned to each one a dependable commander who swore to defend it to the death. Every German soldier in these ports was to fight "to the last man, to the last cartridge."[6] Saint-Malo and Nantes were wrecked, and Brest was so demolished that it was never used as a port by the Allies. Plans to capture Lorient and Saint-Nazaire were abandoned by the Americans, and the German garrisons in both cities held out until the end of the war.[7]

The decision to occupy the channel ports was of the highest strategic importance, John Keegan states in *The Second World War*:

> It lay in the pattern of his [Hitler's] earlier insistence on holding Baltic and Black Sea ports even after their hinterland had fallen to the Red Army, but in this case was far more strongly justified by logistic reality; for, while the Red Army depended scarcely at all upon seaborne supply, the Anglo-American armies did so almost completely. The denial to them of the Channel ports of Le Havre, Boulogne, Calais and Dunkirk gravely impeded their ability to provision their advancing forces and was to have a critical impact on the development of the campaign of liberation throughout the coming autumn and winter.[8]

Hitler's plan was quite successful. With most of the ports closed to the Allies, the bulk of the supplies for Bradley's 12th Army Group had to be delivered over the invasion beaches. As late as July, nearly 90 percent of all materiel was still coming over Omaha and Utah and would continue to enter the ETO over the beaches well into the fall when Antwerp was finally opened to handle cargo. Of a total of 447,000 tons of supplies landed in France between 1 and 25 July, 392,000 tons, or 88 percent, were unloaded over the beaches.[9]

The fact that the armies were being supplied at all, without the expected port capacity, was due in large part to the American "can do" attitude, particularly so because bad weather severely limited unloading operations in the early and late fall.

Throughout most of October, unloading operations were reduced to the point that they barely contributed to the needs of U.S. forces. During the first three weeks of the month, fewer than 25,000 tons per day were unloaded on the continent, but estimated needs exceeded 40,000 tons.[10]

By November, things had improved as discharge capacity increased at Cherbourg and as the ports of Rouen, about

70 miles up the Seine toward Paris, and Le Havre opened for supplies.

The key to relieving Allied supply deficiencies was Antwerp. Located some 70 miles up the Scheldt Estuary, it was one of the world's great ports and, in 1938, had handled twelve thousand ships and some 60 million tons of freight. By late summer 1944, Antwerp was the closest large port to the American lines along the German border in northwest Europe.

Although Antwerp was captured by Montgomery's troops on 4 September, the British field marshal failed to act quickly to clear the enemy from the banks of the Scheldt River, which precipitated one of the great disputes of World War II. Once the Germans had regrouped along the river, Montgomery's Canadian troops struggled for eighty-five days to dislodge the enemy, and ship traffic could not begin to move toward Antwerp until 26 November. By then, it was winter, and the Germans had checked the Allies all along the front. Some observers believe that if Antwerp had been opened shortly after capture, American forces would have had sufficient supplies and gasoline to advance into Germany and end the war in late 1944.

Major General Fuller stated that because the Americans relied so heavily on the Normandy beaches until the opening of Antwerp, "three American divisions had to be 'grounded' near Cherbourg, all their transport being diverted to assist the victorious armies forward."[11]

Fuller, however, faulted the Allied strategy of war more than Montgomery's delay. He speculated why the Allies found themselves in this logistics nightmare:

> The answer is because air power had been so fully exploited strategically and tactically that, when supremacy in the air was assured, it was found that its administrative possibilities had been overlooked. In fact, it had not been grasped that, because the aeroplane can dispense with roads and because it is the most mobile vehicle in existence, it is the ideal supply transporter when cost does not enter into the question. Had fewer bombers

been built, and in their stead had General Eisenhower had at his call, say, two thousand flying four-ton-tankers, there need have been no pausing west of the Rhine, because the northern thrust could have been made in spite of Antwerp, and its flanks could have been protected by aircraft, as Patton's right flank had been in his advance on Paris.[12]

The use of airpower to supply the armies and exploit the German collapse had been only peripherally considered. Instead of thousands of flying tankers, Eisenhower turned to thousands of 2½-ton Jimmies.

The impact of the port problems on the progress of the war was highlighted in early September by Col. William Whipple, chief of the G-4 Logistical Plans Branch at Supreme Headquarters Allied Expeditionary Force (SHAEF) Europe. Whipple noted that, rather than persist in attempting to capture the Breton ports, the Allies should devote their resources to developing the captured Seine ports of Le Havre and Rouen. Ruppenthal noted that by Whipple's estimates, "every 5,000 tons discharged at Le Havre rather than the South Brittany ports . . . would save an equivalent of seventy truck companies."[13]

Nevertheless, the reality in September was that American supply lines stretched some 450 miles from the German frontier to Normandy, and the only way to get supplies to the front was on the Red Ball Express.

SIX

THE RED BALL
GETS ROLLING

The Red Ball Express began its drive into military legend on 25 August 1944. American generals, whose objective just weeks before had been to break out of the Normandy bridgehead, were now more concerned about logistics and supply than about the enemy.

"Logistics—this was the dullest subject in the world," wrote General Bradley. "But logistics were the lifeblood of the Allied armies in France." Bradley and his fellow generals knew that without supplies, "we could not move, shoot, eat."[1]

The appetite of this modern American Army was voracious. Just one U.S. division in combat required 500 tons or more of matériel a day—from ammunition and food to clothing and medical supplies. "With thirty-six divisions in action we were faced with the problem of delivering from beaches and ports to the front lines some 20,000 tons of supplies every day," Eisenhower wrote in *Crusade in Europe*. As more divisions poured into Europe, the need for supplies would only add to the strain of delivering them to the front. "When battling in a fixed position, most of this tonnage is represented in ammunition; on the march the bulk is devoted to gasoline and lubricants, called in the language of the supply officer, POL (petroleum, oil, lubricants)," Eisenhower wrote.[2]

The First and Third Armies each consumed around 400,000 gallons of gas a day as the Shermans advanced out of Normandy.

"Our spearheads . . . were moving swiftly, frequently seventy-five miles per day," Eisenhower wrote. "The supply service had to catch these with loaded trucks. Every mile doubled the difficulty because the supply truck had always to make a two-way run to the beaches and back, in order to deliver another load to the marching troops."[3]

By 4 September, the Third Army front south of the Ardennes was virtually empty of German troops. The Wehrmacht could not stop Patton at this critical juncture, but a shortage of gasoline did.

Ironically, gasoline and other supplies were available in abundance. In Normandy, they were stacked along the sides of the roads, on the beaches, and around the villages, but few supply depots existed between Normandy and the front as the armies pushed forward.

The German Army had learned during the blitzkriegs, in the West in 1940 and in Russia in 1941, that mechanized thrusts outran their supplies and that tanks and their supporting vehicles were at the mercy of their logistics organizations. To supply mechanized forces, particularly with gasoline, in a fast-moving war became a seemingly impossible task. The German panzer forces were so far ahead of the foot-slogging infantry in France in 1940 that military historian Martin Van Creveld believed that this contributed to one of the great strategic blunders of the war. In *Supplying War: Logistics from Wallenstein to Patton*, Van Creveld asserted that the gap between Gen. Heinz Guderian's forward tank formations and the slow-moving German infantry became so wide that the left flank of the German Army advancing through northern France became exposed and vulnerable to attack. This "ultimately contributed to his [Hitler's] decision to halt the tanks short of Dunkirk."[4] Historians have long pondered why Hitler ordered his forces to halt near Dunkirk, which allowed the evacuation of some 337,000 British and French troops to Britain where they were reequipped to fight again. Had Guderian's tanks pressed forward, these men probably would have been captured and the course of the war might have been different.

In addition, the bulk of the German army marched on foot and was supplied by horse and wagon. These slow-moving infantry and supply formations used the same roads as the trucks that supplied the forward mechanized units. The highways became congested by the marching troops and horse-drawn wagons. The Americans avoided road congestion by creating the dedicated Red Ball Highway on which only authorized military vehicles could operate.

Ironically, the success of Allied air attacks during the summer of 1944 hampered the Americans in supplying their armies. The extensive French rail system had been severely damaged so as to prevent the Germans from using trains to support counterattacks against the invasion forces.

The air attacks on the French rail network succeeded beyond the expectations of many in the Allied high command. Rail facilities in Germany long had been targeted in the strategic bombing campaign, but the railroads in northern France became prime targets only two months before D-Day when Eisenhower took command on 14 April 1944 of the strategic air forces in support of the Normandy invasion. The objective of this new mission, according to historian Gordon Harrison, was "to destroy and disrupt the enemy's rail communications, particularly those affecting the enemy's movements towards the 'Overlord' lodgment area."[5]

There was considerable debate about the effectiveness of the bombing plan prior to the invasion. Lt. Gen. Carl Spaatz, commander of the U.S. Eighth Air Force, argued that heavy bombers should focus their attacks on German oil facilities and, in so doing, destroy both valuable petroleum reserves and German fighters. Intelligence studies supported Spaatz and concluded that the German Army used only a small portion of the French rail system and that as much as 90 percent of the system would have to be destroyed to reduce the enemy's ability to respond to the invasion.

Eisenhower believed that even if air attacks had only minimal effect on rail facilities, they could inflict enough damage to prove crucial during the first days and weeks after the invasion when the Allies would be fighting desperately to gain a foothold on French soil. He was right. His strategy, coupled with coordinated ground attacks by the French Resistance, brought the French railroads in Region Nord, the invasion zone, to the point of near collapse, with rail traffic declining by 75 percent between 1 March and D-Day.[6]

The air attacks reached a crescendo on 21 May 1944, dubbed "Chattanooga Day" in the Air Corps. Fighter-bombers, ranging up and down the rail lines, destroyed 50 locomotives and damaged 113 more. Afterward, Generaloberst Friedrich Dollmann, commander of the German Seventh Army, warned Field Marshal Rommel, commander of Army Group B in France, which consisted of the Fifteenth and Seventh Armies, that the new attacks seriously threatened the already strained transportation system.[7]

With the French railroads in shambles, trucks hauled vast quantities of materiel to the front. Cargo manifests from various truck companies tell the story:

- 29 July: Truck companies moved 300,000 gallons of gasoline and 300,000 jerricans from Utah Beach inland to the front.
- 1 August: 400 tons of pipe were transported forward for the POL [gasoline] pipeline being constructed from the beaches to forward depots.
- 1 August: 2,000-gallon semitrailers hauled 380,000 gallons of gasoline from Cherbourg to Beugeville, 1,250,000 gallons of gasoline in jerricans from Omaha Beach to La Haye Pesnil for the Third Army, and 30,000 tons of ammunition to First Army dumps.
- 5 August: 72,000 tons of ammunition were hauled from Omaha Beach to the Saint-Lô area; 600,000 gallons of packaged gas were shipped to the Third Army in forty-eight hours along with 7,400 tons of ammunition to First and Third Army dumps; telephone poles were transported to Cherbourg.[8]

Gasoline was the most critical commodity after the breakout. The Shermans alone guzzled fuel at a rate of one gallon per 1–2 miles during combat. In the logistical calculations for the armies, a quarter of all supplies needed to sustain the drive into Germany was in the form of petroleum products, mostly gasoline.[9]

As early as 14 June 1944, the American Army had opened what could be considered the first of its express highway routes— the POL routes on the continent that were continued until the end of the war. POL trucks, mostly 750- and 2,000-gallon tankers, hauled gasoline and oil products from distribution points along the POL pipelines that were being constructed from the beachhead to inland depots. Other trucks picked up gas, much of it packaged in jerricans, at various captured ports along the English Channel and hauled it forward. Once the Red Ball was established, POL trucks often followed the Red Ball route.

Even with the quantities of POL and other supplies reaching the front during the early days of the pursuit, the armies needed much more than was being delivered, particularly after Eisenhower approved the attack eastward beyond the Seine. In response, the American Army created the Red Ball Express in an effort to create orderly and efficient operations and to increase the amount of materiel reaching the combat troops.

The Red Ball was established thirty-six hours after Allied commanders huddled to find a solution to the growing supply crisis. The principals in the planning process were two officers in COMZ headquarters, Lt. Col. Loren A. Ayers, chief of MTB, and Maj. Gordon K. Gravelle. Their quick thinking, literally overnight, launched one of the more critical operations in the ETO and created an enduring military legend.

Red Ball was a common railway term in the 1940s that had the same meaning as today's express mail. Before the creation of the famous Red Ball Express in August 1944, an initial Red Ball had been established in Great Britain just after D-Day to send urgently needed supplies across the channel to the Normandy front. Invasion planners had estimated the supply needs of the invasion forces months in advance of the cross-channel attack, and all the materiel that was required in the first days and weeks after the assault was preloaded on ships of the invasion fleet. But once ashore, the attacking forces often needed supplies that had not been anticipated, and the first Red Ball was established as a "special delivery" service in which 100 tons of shipping space was set aside each day to meet emergency requests from France.[10]

By 25 August 1944, it had become apparent that another Red Ball Express was needed to get supplies to the front as the Allies pursued the Germans inland. The plan conceived by Ayers and Gravelle called for the pooling of as many COMZ and MTB trucks and facilities as possible. It also called for the requisition of nonessential trucks from units throughout the Army's forces in the ETO. Vehicles were taken from antiaircraft units, artillery battalions, engineer companies, and even from newly arrived infantry divisions awaiting transfer to the front.

A major problem facing the Americans at this point was a critical shortage of Jimmies and tractor-trailers to do the job. Prior to the invasion, Allied transportation planners had requested 240 trucking companies to serve the needs of the large American expeditionary force that, by mid-August, was approaching twenty divisions and totaling about a million men. Because of the worldwide conflict, however, the War Department was able to allocate only 160 truck companies to the ETO. Even with its vast industrial capacity, the United States could not produce enough trucks to meet demand. In addition to trucks manufactured for U.S. forces, scores of thousands of Jimmies were being shipped to the Soviet Union under the Lend-Lease program. Trucks were also sent by the thousands to the Mediterranean Theater, the Pacific Theater, and remote bases all over the world.

Eisenhower's staff requested that a preponderance of trucks in the ETO be tractor-trailers that could haul from 7 to 10 tons in each load, twice that of the Jimmy. The tractor-trailers made round-trips more rapidly because they could drop off the trailers, hook up to empty ones, and head back without waiting to be unloaded. But production of these trucks lagged, and worldwide considerations precluded delivery of more of them to the ETO. During the summer and fall of 1944, the Red Ball Express would have to get by mostly with Jimmies.

On its inaugural day, the Red Ball was launched with 67 truck companies and 3,358 trucks, the majority Jimmies, and hauled 4,482 tons of supplies on the 125-mile run to Chartres. By the fourth day of operations, the number of truck companies had nearly doubled to 132, employing 5,958 vehicles to deliver more than 12,000 tons of supplies. The Americans were establishing a new system of depots in the Chartres-Dreux area to supply U.S. forces advancing beyond the Seine toward Germany. Red Ball trucks were stacked high with all the accoutrements of war as they poured out of the lush Norman countryside toward the spires of Chartres.[11]

Veterans of the campaigns in Normandy and northern France remembered the Red Ball Express from the endless stream of trucks bumping past on the one-way route, often so overloaded with supplies that ammunition and ration boxes sometimes bounced out as the Jimmies hit potholes or negotiated turns. Many of the trucks were marked with red ball symbols on the front bumpers, and the engineers made road signs with large red balls centered on white placards to designate the Red Ball Highway. Engineers also made thousands of "one-way" signs and signs warning unauthorized vehicles to "keep off" in order to prevent French drivers and nonauthorized military vehicles from using the highway.

The Red Ball quickly developed a reputation for highway bravado. Speeding was commonplace, and a wrecked Jimmy near a sharp curve or at the bottom of a hill was a common sight along the road leading to Germany. One motto of the Red Ball came from a French phrase adopted by the Americans—*tout de suite* (immediately, right now). "Patton wanted us to eat, sleep, and drive, but mostly drive," said John O'Leary of the 3628th QM Truck Company.[12]

Even the British remembered the Red Ball. It became a standard joke among the Tommies that if they saw an American Red

Ball truck barreling down the road, they should jump out of the way and try to climb a tree. The Brits weren't the only ones who ran. French civilians also knew to get out of the way. Red Ball veteran Earl "Red" Swallow, who volunteered as a driver from the 102d Infantry Division, wrote that he "drove on the narrow streets of St. Lo and came down a hill where the road turned sharp right. Many people were riding bicycles and as I turned the corner I was a bit up on the sidewalk causing one bike rider to dart into the nearest open doorway."[13]

Roy Benner, a Red Ball veteran, recalled not only the speed but the noise of the Red Ball across the French countryside. "Most of the Red Ball truck mufflers got holes in them. . . . Sure did sound powerful going through the narrow roads in the French towns, especially at night."[14]

The original Red Ball route was a loop road that ran one way to Chartres on one designated highway and back, one way, on another. The French road system was so clogged with American military vehicles that had the Red Ball route not been a dedicated, one-way highway, the convoys would have quickly become bogged down in traffic.

Compared with the roads in the bridgehead, portions of the Red Ball Highway were exceedingly well built. *Routes nationales*— the French equivalent of federal highways in the United States— over which many of the trucks ran, varied from 20 to 26 feet in width and dated from the Napoleonic era when they had been constructed of granite blocks. Literally, they were solid as rock and almost indestructible. *Chemins départementaux*—equivalent to state roads in the United States—were not as well constructed and ranged in width from 10 to 20 feet, but they were adequate.

Even though its primary mission was to haul gasoline, rations, and ammunition, the Red Ball carried everything imaginable as it rolled on. "We carried anything from straight pins to tank parts, and we carried them in all kinds of conditions and all kinds of weather," James Rookard said.[15]

Nonessential goods were often shipped with critical military items because the Army wanted supplies to get to the front as quickly as possible. Depot personnel had a tendency to throw anything on a truck—including brooms, soft drinks, even fly swatters.[16]

One driver remembered the loads that he carried:

> I hauled potatoes to a little town called Beauvais; I hauled flour to a bakery some place; I hauled Coca-Cola to Brussels, Belgium, when they started up the bottling plant there; I hauled rolls of reenforcing wire; I hauled metal plates, wood decking, mostly ammo and gasoline. I believe I might have hauled more gasoline than anything.[17]

Another driver hauled 20 tons of yellow soap to a destination in northern Europe. "Our first bit of cargo was a truck full of large tin containers of hard candy," Red Swallow wrote.[18]

Red Ball trucks even carried bridges. The principal mission of the 3603d QM Truck Company on the Red Ball during October was to haul Bailey bridges forward to river crossings on 40-foot trailers. The Bailey, a British invention, came in transportable sections that could be quickly connected by engineers. The biggest problem faced by the trucking units that transported the sections was getting them through the twisting, narrow streets of villages that straddled the roadway.

The Red Ball Highway, in its first days, began in Saint-Lô, the dispatching point for outbound convoys, and ran south to Vire and Domfront, southeast to Couptrain, and east to Alençon, Montagne, and La Loupe to terminate in the Chartres area. The return leg ran from Chartres west to Nogent-le-Rotrou, Bellême, Mamers, Villaines-la-Juhel, Mayenne, Mortain, Tessy-sur-Vire, and back to Saint-Lô. The total length of the outbound and inbound routes was some 300 miles.

Although the Red Ball Highway technically began at Saint-Lô, trucks often traveled north through the Cotentin Peninsula to pick up supplies on the invasion beaches. During the breakout, Saint-Lô, the regional capital of the Department of La Manche at the neck of the Cotentin Peninsula, had been

bombed and shelled into mounds of rubble so wide and so deep
that traffic-directing MPs restricted trucks to one lane on many
streets in the city to prevent the outbound and inbound convoys
from getting tangled.

"There was just enough room on the streets of Saint-Lô to get
one truck through," recounted Phillip Dick, a scout corporal in
an artillery unit assigned to temporary duty on the Red Ball.
"The town was totally smashed."[19]

The historian of the 513th Truck Regiment noted that "the
dust, swirling about us as the convoy rode through Saint-Lô,
completely covered vehicles and personnel and it was hardly
possible to see to drive through. Bridges, which had been blown
or destroyed had to be bypassed through fields where cattle lay
dead and decaying in the heat of the day."[20]

Beyond Saint-Lô and all along the Red Ball Highway, especially during the first days of the operation, were signs of battle—
German tanks, trucks, and command cars pushed to the sides of
the roads or resting askew in the fields, all victims of furious
Allied air attacks, and occasional graves of fallen Wehrmacht
soldiers.

"We continued through Vire, Mortain, Domfront, Couptrain,
Pre-en-Pail. All bore the evidence of the swirling whirlpool of
war in more or less degree. Vire was worse, if possible, than
Saint-Lô," Eugene V. Diemer, author of *The History of the 513th
Quartermaster Group (TC)*, noted.[21]

Once out of Saint-Lô, the convoys moved more rapidly
through the Norman countryside that, during the last days of
August, gave off heavy and rich smells of sweet grass and drying
wheat, much of it in great rolls lying in the fields. The landscape
was a tableau of dark greens on the wooded hillsides and golds in
the rolling wheatfields below. Dotting every hill crest were apple
orchards where Norman farmers produced their world-famous
cider. The troops particularly liked the hard cider.

Farmsteads, with ancient and flaking walls, hugged the roads,
and the exhaust fumes from thousands of six-cylinder Jimmies
mixed with the pungent odor of cow manure in the fields. Every

few miles were villages of clustered stone cottages, their stuccoed walls weathered to a drab putty color and their weary appearance, accentuated by the typical shuttered windows, offset by the bright orange of the tiled roofs.

When the trucks entered the small villages along the route, the Red Ball convoys were often reduced to a crawl. For the larger trucks, the 10-ton tractor-trailers stacked high with gas-filled jerricans, it took all the skill of their drivers to maneuver them through the maze of narrow streets. Even the smaller six-by-six Jimmies, with their 1-ton trailers, often found the going difficult within the narrow spaces of villages built during the Middle Ages.

Houdan, even older, was a truck transfer point on the road to Chartres that had been inhabited since Roman times. Narrow streets wound around timbered houses, an ancient church in the center of the village, and a dungeon near the outskirts of town.

Once the Red Ball route left the coastal areas, the convoys hurried through a flat and open plain that resembled parts of the American West, with the sky a blue dome on bright, clear days. The trucks rolled on, under canopies of sycamore trees, past green fields blanketed with yellow flowers and the tall stalks of sunflowers. Always in the distance was another village and the ubiquitous concrete water towers to supply villages and farms. Many towers had been destroyed by Allied fighters because they had served as German observation points.

Soon the spires of Chartres came into view across a wide plain. For some drivers on the Red Ball, the ancient cathedral was an exhilarating sight. Chartres was the final destination point of the Red Ball during its first days, and Phillip Dick used the bell towers as reference points to guide his convoy, just as peasants had done centuries before during the Middle Ages. With the title of "scout corporal," Dick was often expected to be the navigator and keep the convoy on course. Once the cathedral was visible, he could not make a mistake.

Trucks by the thousands were rolling through the days and nights out of Normandy and Saint-Lô. The need for supplies was so great that COMZ permitted trucks to travel with headlights ablaze after dark in areas 10 or more miles from the front if the convoy commander thought it prudent, although many convoys still used only the cat eyes. In a world where darkness had enveloped Europe every night for nearly five years, the head-lights of Red Ball trucks were a strange experience to the French. One Red Ball driver was startled to see a woman, screaming with delight, rush from her home as his convoy drove through her village with headlights on full. For an instant, she had believed that the war was over.

In the new, mechanized American Army in the ETO, the Red Ball route was often used to transport troops. Entire formations were shifted by truck to new battle zones, and replacements were rushed in to fill the ranks of depleted combat units. The Third Army began trucking troops into combat early in the breakout, particularly in Brittany. These were the first of many operations in which armored forces, infantry, and truck drivers worked together.[22]

During the Brittany campaign, the 514th Truck Regiment transported elements of the 90th and 79th Infantry Divisions into action. The truckers stayed with the troops and moved them forward with every advance. Historian Sarah Davis noted that the truckers "were with the infantry night and day—eating, fighting and digging in—taking enemy sniping during the day and aerial bombing and strafing at night."[23] Trucks made it possible for the 30th Division to advance 118 miles to Tournai, Belgium, in thirty hours.

As the war progressed, the cooperative effort between trucks and infantry was streamlined. In early October, I Company trucks made a 400-mile trek along the Red Ball from the Nancy area back to Cherbourg to move the recently arrived 26th Division to the front. The job of ferrying troops around the European Theater had become so routine that Corporal Brice devoted only one line in his history to the move.

Sometimes there were surprises in the movement of troops. The 146th QM Truck Company was ordered to a port area to transport newly arrived GIs to more forward areas. Jim Brown, a driver with the 146th, remembered that it was pitch dark when the trucks arrived at the loading point:

> You couldn't see nothing—no lights of any kind. We were loading troops on the trailers with helmets and packs. You don't drive with lights, there's no one sitting up front with you, so come daylight they said, well we gotta stop, give the troops a break. So this girl gets out, she's a Colonel! She says "Alright the girls on this side, the boys on that side." Here was a general hospital we had picked up and all those things we were hoisting up in those trucks were women. We didn't know it, the girls didn't say anything. Nobody said anything. We just shoved 'em on up and shut the tailgate. I don't know how many nurses we carried, but it was a whole damn convoy.[24]

But life on the Red Ball soon became routine for many of the drivers, including Fred Cox, a driver with the 146th:

> From day-to-day, follow the leader. The sergeant gets in the front truck and other trucks follow. After a while you get to know those roads. There was a certain road we'd take if we was going up toward the front and we'd come back on another road which on the Red Ball you were supposed to do.[25]

Historian Bass also wrote of the daily grind on the Red Ball that quickly dulled men's senses:

> We were based alongside the road at a little town called Pontchartrain which wasn't too far from Versailles which wasn't too far from Paris which didn't mean a damned thing to us because all we did was go around "the loop." Wherever we were assigned. We didn't know where the hell we were going or what we were doing. We just did what we were told and followed the truck in front and hoped the guy knew where he was going. We went through some rough places at times and then

we'd go back the return route to Rouen, load up again, come back the eastern route by our base camp in Pontchartrain and the driver and the assistant driver and the maintenance crew would get off and a fresh crew and fresh maintenance crew would take over and they would make the round trip."[26]

Even the great landmarks of Europe elicited little response from the men in the trucks. Bass remarked on the reaction of many drivers as they passed the ancient cathedral of Chartres: "So what!"

THE BLOOD OF WAR

The French called it *le sang rouge de guerre*—the red blood of war. The British called it petrol. The Americans called it gasoline, but in the waning days of August 1944, it might as well have been gold.

"'If I could only steal some gas, I could win this war,' Patton complained to me," Bradley wrote in his memoirs, *A General's Life*. "'Damn it, Brad, just give me 400,000 gallons of gasoline and I'll put you inside Germany in two days.' He might as well have asked for the moon."[1]

The availability of gasoline was not a problem when the Allies were contained in Normandy. Even after the breakout and during the early weeks of the pursuit, they had enough gas. The First and Third Armies were operating close together, and their supply lines back to the Normandy beaches and ports stretched no more than 150 miles. But once beyond the Seine, the armies fanned out. The First Army thrust north into Belgium as the Third Army moved southeast toward Metz and Verdun, only 50 miles from the German frontier. The wings of the two armies were between 50 and 75 miles apart in early August, but they were as much as 200 miles apart in early September, and each was more than 400 miles from Normandy.

The amount of gasoline required to continue the pursuit boggled the minds of Army logisticians. They had studied the Meuse-Argonne offensive of World War I when American forces consumed 150,000 gallons of gas during the entire operation, an enormous expenditure at the time.[2] By late August 1944, the First and Third Armies together were consuming an average of more than 800,000 gallons a day and, on 24 August, the First Army alone burned 782,000 gallons.

On August 26, both the First and Third Armies reported less than one day's supply on hand, and, on 28 August, the Third Army reported a shortfall of nearly 100,000 gallons. The next day's deliveries fell short by 141,520 gallons of the 325,000 gallons requested. During the first week of September, deliveries fell to "token size, totaling a mere 31,975, 25,390, and 49,930 gallons on 30 August and 2 and 3 September respectively."[3]

By the first week in September, gasoline supplies for U.S. mechanized forces had dwindled to such dangerously low levels and the situation was becoming so desperate that Red Ball trucks often drove right past the forward depots and delivered jerricans to the tanks within yards of enemy lines. The histories of the pursuit are highlighted with stories of the Red Ball trucks delivering gas to the front. Washington Rector, a truck driver with the 3916th QM Truck Company, took supplies "right up to the tanks." The landscape was peppered with shell holes, and the dead had yet to be retrieved by Graves Registration.[4]

Stars and Stripes, the Army newspaper, praised these Red Ball drivers: "We often refuel and rearm even while fighting. That takes guts. Our Negro outfits delivered gas under constant fire. Damned if I'd want their job. They have what it takes."[5]

John Shevlin, an assistant tank driver in the Fifth Armored Division, lauded the bravery of Red Ball drivers at the height of the pursuit: "If it wasn't for the Red Ball we couldn't have moved. They all were black drivers and they delivered in the heat of combat. We'd be in our tanks praying for them to come up."[6]

Despite the gas shortages, Patton fought on. When he learned that his XII Corps commander, Maj. Gen. Manton Eddy, had halted at Saint-Dizier on the Marne River to conserve gas, the Third Army commander was outraged. "You get off your fanny as fast as you can and move on until your engines run dry, and then move forward on foot, Goddamnit," Patton bellowed at Eddy.[7]

Also, Patton was furious at Montgomery, whom he accused of taking the Third Army's fuel allocations. With an adequate supply, Patton believed, he could end the war. Whether he could have smashed his way to Berlin is open to question, but it generates intriguing debate about how the war might have been fought—and won.

Patton found gas by hook or crook. The Third had been able to reach the Meuse because Patton's men had captured a million gallons of German petrol. It was of low quality, but it worked and kept the tanks advancing. Yet it was not enough to keep the Third rolling for long, and Patton's troops began commandeering gasoline wherever they found it. Charles Stevenson, a lieutenant with the 3858th QM Gas Supply Company, led a gasoline convoy that was stopped by Third Army gas pirates. An officer stood in the middle of the road and said the trucks could not move until each driver turned over his cargo of jerricans. Stevenson refused. "We fussed, jumped up and down and cussed him out and raised hell and damned him to hell. But he said that won't do you any good. Just give us the jerricans." Stevenson begged that his men be allowed to keep enough gas to return to base, and the request was granted.[8]

Many thieves were not so accommodating. They took every drop from trucks and convoys and even spare jerricans that were to be used to get the trucks and convoys back to base. In consequence, entire convoys were often left stranded and required added manpower and gasoline to get them back on the road.[9]

Stevenson's company commander engaged in another heated argument with a full colonel from the Third Army who was at the head of a hijacking contingent. The colonel ordered the captain to turn over every jerrican in the convoy.

"No way, buddy, this is our basic load [a basic load was 125 jerricans] and we're going through," the captain told the colonel. The argument raged, but the colonel prevailed.

"The guy who argued the longest, loudest and hardest, won," Stevenson said.[10]

Patton encouraged his troops to go to great lengths to "requisition" gasoline. They hijacked trucks destined for Paris and siphoned off fuel from First Army dumps. The officer in charge of securing supplies for the Third Army was Col. Walter J. Muller, Patton's assistant chief of staff for supplies. Muller's scavenger hunts made him an army legend.[11]

"There was rumor," Patton later wrote with tongue in cheek, "which, officially, I hoped was not true, that some of our Ordnance people passed themselves off as members of the First Army and secured quite a bit of gasoline from one of the dumps of that unit. To reverse the statement made about the Light Brigade, this is not war but is magnificent."[12]

In a letter of 30 August 1994 to his wife, Beatrice, Patton admitted that his troops were stealing gas. "Sad to say a colored truck company did steal some for me by careful accident."[13] Needless to say, his thieving truckers were not disciplined.

Devious ways usually have been ascribed to the Third Army in the mythology of World War II, but the First Army resorted to thievery as well. The only difference was that Patton's exploits were more adventurous and often more outrageous than Hodges's and made better headlines. Historian Ladislas Farago noted that the First Army quartermaster used scout planes to search for additional stocks, and the Fifth Armored Division also resorted to hijacking gasoline stores.[14]

Blumenson wrote that even General Bradley succumbed to the need to snitch gasoline:

> Bradley, whose innate modesty and fairness somewhat tempered his predatory sense, esteemed his longtime G-4, Colonel [Robert W.] Wilson, with the smug pride Fagin regarded his flock of little pickpockets. Maintaining that all was fair in love and war, Bradley praised Wilson for developing chicanery into a high art in the business of supplies. "He fully merited his reputation for piracy," Bradley gleefully said.[15]

At the core of the shortage was the Red Ball Express. There could be no gas without the Red Ball, yet the Red Ball consumed so much fuel that it made the problem worse. It probably is no coincidence that the worst of the crisis occurred during the last week of August and the first week of September, the startup weeks of the Red Ball. Red Ball trucks daily consumed more than 300,000 gallons just to get to the front.

The situation was aggravated after Paris was liberated on 25 August. During the invasion planning, the French capital was not slated for liberation until October because logisticians knew that vast amounts of materiel would have to be diverted from the front to sustain the city's population. But Paris was the symbol of France's resurrection and was too tempting for French Gen. Charles de Gaulle and Maj. Gen. Phillip Leclerc to ignore. Leclerc dispatched a small force of light tanks, armored cars, and personnel carriers to the city, ostensibly to find the most suitable route into the capital. The real reason, however, was that Leclerc wanted his Free French troops to be the first Allied soldiers into Paris. Eisenhower finally authorized the change of plans and allowed the French to liberate the city.[16]

Ernie Pyle reported that Paris seemed unchanged after four years of occupation but noted that the people were impoverished and hungry. "If you were to take a poll on what the average Parisian wants after four years in the way of little things you'd find that he wants real coffee, soap, gas and cigarettes."[17] The Allies complied and immediately began supplying Paris with shipments totaling 23,000 tons of food. The deliveries included wine, which had been scarce during the war.

When there was insufficient motor transport to move the supplies into Paris, Eisenhower ordered C-47s to supplement the railroads and trucks. The brunt of the work, however, fell to the Red Ball. Supplying the Parisians took hundreds of trucks and thousands of gallons of gasoline.[18]

The Parisians were not the only ones diverting the precious gas stocks and vehicles from the front. Gen. John C. H. Lee, commanding general of COMZ, decided to move his vast headquarters from Cherbourg to Paris. The move consumed 25,000 gallons of gasoline and also diverted trucks to haul all the supplies. Once in Paris, Lee's officers and men also commandeered most of the hotel space in the city. Lee earned the enmity of the generals, including Eisenhower.[19]

Gasoline was being moved to the front by every means possible, including flights of C-47s. The Americans also were constructing a system of pipelines from Cherbourg east toward Paris to carry gas to forward depots where it could be dispensed into jerricans or into tanker trucks that would move it to the front. But the engineers could not build the pipeline fast enough. As much as 30 miles of 6-inch pipeline was laid in a single day, but the advance of 40 miles or more a day during the pursuit often outpaced construction. Use of the pipeline was also hampered because the line never could be filled. It was always being emptied through distribution into jerricans and tanker trucks at points farther to the rear. At one point on 13 September, it was estimated that the pipeline contained 200,000 barrels of gasoline.[20]

The railroads were smashed, the POL pipeline could not dispense gasoline fast enough during the pursuit to meet the needs of the fast-moving Shermans, and the ports that could take gasoline tankers were demolished or in German hands. So how were the American armies supplied with gas? For the most part, it came in the 5-gallon jerrican that reached the front lines on the Red Ball Express.

EIGHT

OVER THE BEACHES, INTO THE MUD

For months after D-Day, despite the usual snafus, debris of war, and a storm-lashed English Channel, supplies continued to arrive over the Normandy beaches without letup. Stubby little DUKWs (pronounced ducks), amphibious versions of the 2½-ton truck, were hard at work ferrying in supplies, including hundreds of thousands of loaded jerricans, from ships at anchor in and around the Mulberry harbor. They chugged through the artificial harbor to lug their cargoes onto the beaches to hastily improvised supply dumps in the hedgerows that were little more than piles of rations, ammunition boxes, and 5-gallon containers. Once ashore, the landlubbing Jimmies were loaded and dispatched to the front or to newly established depots inland.

The artificial Mulberry harbor, carefully designed and constructed, consisted of a series of massive blocks of concrete, each one the size of a small city block. These "blockships" had been fabricated at ports around Great Britain, floated across the channel, and sunk in place off the invasion beaches just after D-Day. Once in position, they formed a small harbor and breakwater. They were connected to shore by a 2,450-foot pontoon causeway on which trucks could drive out and take on loads from freighters and tankers docked alongside the pier.

The Mulberry harbor was destroyed by a severe storm that raged through the channel on June 19–22. The blockships were scattered in the shallow waters off the invasion beaches and soon added to the debris of wrecked landing craft, sunken ships, ruined trucks and armored vehicles, and German obstacles that littered the shoreline and the water several hundred yards out to sea.

The storm made the slow and cumbersome unloading process even more so. In desperation, Army engineers cut open the hulls of wrecked and beached ships and removed the cargoes.[1] Bulldozers cut paths through the debris on the beaches and opened new roads inland to speed the unloading process.

Initially, the Navy refused to allow its LSTs (landing ships, tank) to dock at the water's edge in fear that the vessels would break in two as they settled on the uneven beach. The exigencies of war prevailed, however, and the vessels were beached with no adverse effects. Trucks could drive up the bow ramps into the hulls of the LSTs and load supplies. When an LST was empty, it floated back out to sea at high tide.

Despite the need for haste and efficiency, Red Ball trucks often were idle, sometimes for days, as they lined up to wait for loading. Drivers milled about or slept in their cabs to make up for the hours on the road. One Red Ball veteran was startled to see General Patton arrive and admonish a young lieutenant for allowing the trucks to remain bunched in the open. Patton jumped down from his command car and strutted up to the quivering officer, who attempted a smart salute. "Who the hell's in charge of this Goddam mess?" Patton demanded to know. "One Jerry coming down here with a plane could wipe out that highway."[2]

All supplies were categorized in a classification system, and supply depots often had specialized functions relating to the class of supplies they received. Gasoline dumps were the most common specialized depots.

Class I supplies were those that the Army knew would be consumed at a uniform rate, principally rations. Class II included clothing and weapons; Class III consisted of gasoline, lubricating oils, and other petroleum products; Class IV was a miscellaneous category for such things as construction materiel; and Class V included ammunition, explosives, and chemical agents.[3]

Commanders prodded their men to get the trucks back on the road as quickly as possible. One Army analysis of sixteen Red Ball convoys (a convoy usually consisted of about sixteen to twenty trucks) revealed that the fastest loading time for one was eleven and a half hours. For six of the convoys, it took fifteen to twenty hours to load; for five of the convoys, loading time was up to thirty hours; and for two of the convoys, the time was thirty-four and thirty-nine hours, respectively. In this war of movement, in which the forward combat units were sometimes advancing scores of miles a day, the dispatch time for supplies to the front was extremely slow.[4]

Things were not much better at the depots near the front. A time analysis at one depot showed that the fastest unloading operation among sixteen convoys was eleven hours. Some of the convoys required unloading times of fifteen to twenty hours, while others required thirty-five to thirty-six hours, respectively.[5]

The irony was that frontline troops could unload much more quickly by unloading one truck right into another. A Red Ball truck that had bypassed a forward supply depot would back up against another from an infantry or armored unit, and troops would shift and slide the cargoes from one truck bed to another. The newly loaded trucks would then become rolling supply dumps that followed the troops wherever they went.

Incessant rain during the summer of 1944 seriously slowed the loading process. Rains produced seas of mud around the supply dumps, and the beach and inland depots were mired in it as the trucks moved to and fro each day.

"You'd go in and load up [at a depot] and if you had any trouble the dozer'd start pushing you," recalled several drivers with the 146th QM Truck Company. "You had a dozer pushing trucks into the warehouse and a crane pulling because the mud was so deep and when you stepped out of the truck . . . you were up to your knees in mud. . . . "[6]

German prisoners of war (POWs) were used as stevedores to help speed the flow of supplies over the beaches and this was where many American GIs had their first glimpses of the enemy.

Nearly every rear-echelon unit used prisoners to load and unload trucks and DUKWs. As the pursuit continued, POWs became an important manpower source to keep the Allied armies supplied. Some companies had as few as six POWs, whereas others had up to several hundred.

C Company, like many of the units on the Red Ball, had a group of POWs assigned for work details, often KP (kitchen police) duty. POWs also refueled the trucks and loaded vehicles. James Chappelle said that the Germans assigned to C Company did not seem eager to escape and were loosely guarded. Most had no desire to return to the war, and some in the civilian populations of France and Belgium harbored such hatred toward "les Boches" that they might have killed any escaped POWs they captured.

At one service station operated by the 3939th Gas Supply Company in Reims, France, as many as 250 German POWs checked tire pressure and oil levels and cleaned windshields of hundreds of Jimmies that pulled in for refueling.

Some POWs were not eager to help the Americans. Numerous Red Ball veterans saw prisoners dragging open jerricans through rain and snow to contaminate the gasoline with water. Jimmies were particularly vulnerable to fuel line freezing, which made it nearly impossible to start the vehicles. Charles Stevenson said that sometimes the only way to get his Jimmies going on wintry mornings was to heat the fuel lines with an acetylene torch. It was a dangerous practice but effective.[7]

POWs also found ways to avoid working. One company's contingent of prisoners disappeared for several hours. A search discovered them hiding among ammunition boxes and snacking on peanut butter and jelly crackers that they had pilfered from nearby ration crates.

NINE

STRANGERS IN WHITE AMERICA

What you doin' on the Red Ball, soldier, you ain't no nigger?"[1]

Robert Emerick often got this type of comment from white soldiers when they learned that he was a driver on the Red Ball Express. The comments meant nothing to Emerick, but to African Americans, such as James Rookard, racial slurs stung and were common in the Army. "The Caucasians brought their prejudices with them, even in war," Rookard said.[2]

If such epithets reflected the virulent prejudices of many American soldiers during World War II, they were at least backhanded acknowledgements of the contributions made by the hundreds of thousands of African American soldiers who served in the war. Not only did they make up the majority of men on the Red Ball but also the majority of personnel on the later express trucking lines that carried supplies for the Army all the way to the Elbe River deep in Germany.

The men of C Company were typical of the black troops in Red Ball trucking units who almost universally came from economically disadvantaged families. James Chappelle grew up in Cleveland and dropped out of high school in the eleventh grade to go to work. Rookard, who never knew his father and grew up in Cleveland tenements, also dropped out of high school. More than half of the blacks in the Army were from poor, rural districts in the South.

Lt. Col. John H. Sherman, a white officer who commanded African American troops during the war, made the following observation about them:

> About six-sevenths of the Negro troops come from areas in which equal educational opportunities, equal pay for equal work and opportunity to work at skilled trades are denied them. So far as it can be accomplished, pride and self-respect also are denied them by political discrimination, social ostracism and the common use of epithets which pound into most of them a hopeless feeling of inferiority. While a large proportion have good basic intelligence, they are drastically handicapped by the lack of even elementary schooling. They were taken from school as soon as they were old enough to pick berries, chop cotton, weed onions, hoe corn, pick cotton or slash tobacco.[3]

African Americans had established a proud tradition in the U.S. Army since the Revolution, when some 5,000 of them served in the Continental Army, many in integrated companies. But that was the last time until the Korean War that blacks fought shoulder to shoulder with whites. During the 175-year period from 1775 until 1950, black troops were relegated to segregated units, and most of these were service units, particularly during World Wars I and II.

An estimated 186,000 African Americans enlisted in the Union Army during the Civil War. In 1866 the Army organized two all-black cavalry regiments, the 9th and 10th Cavalry Regiments. Sent out West to fight in the Indian Wars, these troopers were the first African American soldiers to be called "Buffalo Soldiers," an Indian term of respect that was subsequently applied to other black Indian-fighting soldiers and their descendant units. In 1869, the Army's four all-black infantry regiments were consolidated into the 24th and 25th Infantry Regiments. The cavalry, especially, became one place in the Army where blacks were recognized in the American military.[4]

The 9th and 10th Cavalry Regiments and the 24th and 25th Infantry Regiments served in Cuba during the Spanish-American War in 1898 and distinguished themselves at San Juan Hill and El Caney. During the twentieth century, however, racism intensified and blacks were excluded from participating in mainstream Army life. Two black combat units, the 92d and 93d Infantry Divisions, served in World War I, but they were poorly led and not highly regarded by the American high command.

The black troops who served in World War II were only a couple of generations removed from the Buffalo Soldiers. To many African American recruits in 1943, these former Indian fighters were their heroes. Rookard wasn't alone in imagining himself as a cavalryman dressed smartly in Army blues and riding a sleek stallion. "That uniform! Every young fella wanted to be in the cavalry."

After being drafted, Rookard was sent to Fort Hays in Columbus, Ohio, where the nucleus of C Company was forming. He joined other blacks from northern Ohio—Chappelle, Marvin Hall, Charles Fletcher, James Bailey, and Fred Newton.

C Company's stay at Fort Hays was short lived. Wearing Army denims and floppy hats, the men were packed into trains and shipped to Fort Meade, where their black officers were reassigned and white officers took command. It long had been Army policy that whites commanded in most African American units, in part, because the Army believed that blacks did not trust or respect black officers. The majority of the whites in command of the blacks were southerners because the Army believed that they knew better how to deal with blacks.

Generally, the men of C Company tolerated their white officers throughout the war. In some cases, there was genuine, mutual respect and amity, but there was also animus. Rookard recalled one white officer who had no interest in commanding black troops. "My name is Captain Roberts, and I'm from Alabama," he bellowed at his introduction during a company formation. Roberts emphasized the word Alabama, and the men of C Company had no illusions about Roberts's racial attitudes.[5]

One white commanding officer spoke of his black troops as though they were children. "I think the brightest one had an IQ of about one hundred. The average was around eighty. Many of them couldn't read or write. But they were street smart, country street smart," the officer said. He used the term *country* because most of the troops in his unit came from farming families in the Carolinas.[6]

Soon after arriving at Fort Meade, Rookard and his comrades learned that they would attain no glory in this war. They were assigned as truck drivers. The fighting would be left to whites.

To be sure, there were all-black combat units, the most famous of which was the 332d Fighter Group, the Tuskegee Airmen, commanded by Col. Benjamin O. Davis, a West Point graduate who later retired as an Air Force lieutenant general. The record of the 332d was exemplary. The largest of the all-black combat units were the 92d and 93d Infantry Divisions, first organized in World War I and reactivated in World War II. The fighting qualities of the men in these two divisions during World War I were generally praised in the press and by the French Army under which many of the black troops served. The French government awarded the Croix de Guerre to three regiments of the 93d. Nevertheless, the American high command didn't think much of its black combat troops.

Between the two world wars, the Army continued to believe that blacks didn't measure up in combat. "The War Department's resistance to employing black men in combat stemmed in part from the stereotypical belief that black men were inferior to white men," Professor Brenda L. Moore wrote in *To Serve My Country, To Serve My Race*.[7]

Historian Ulysses Grant Lee noted this attitude in his work, *The Employment of Negro Troops*:

Relying heavily on testimony by World War I commanders of the Ninety-Second and Ninety-Third divisions, military officials supported the notion that black men should be used "principally as labor organizations." The [white] commander of the

367th Infantry [92d Division] is cited as stating, "As fighting troops, the Negro must be rated as second class material; this is due primarily to his inferior intelligence and lack of mental and moral qualities."[8]

Lee quotes from a letter written by the Army's chief historian, Dr. Walter L. Wright, Jr., concerning the plight of black troops:

> American Negro troops are . . . ill-educated on the average and often illiterate; they lack self-respect, self-confidence, and initiative; they tend to be very conscious of their low standing in the eyes of the white population and consequently feel very little motive for aggressive fighting. . . . After all, when a man knows that the color of his skin will automatically disqualify him from reaping the fruits of attainment it is no wonder that he sees little point in trying very hard to excel anybody else."[9]

In a post–World War II assessment, the Army admitted that the 694,818 African American troops who served during the war were largely ignored, and the prime reason was that they served in service units that received none of the press coverage of combat units.[10]

Nevertheless, their contribution to the war effort was extensive. Lee noted that there were more than four thousand small segregated units employed all over the world:

> The variety in the employment of Negro troops so far outstripped anything seen in World War I or contemplated at the beginning of World War II that this fact alone is of prime significance in any account of the use of Negro troops in World War II. The sheer quantity of work performed by Negro units, often operating on round-the-clock schedules, was tremendous. . . . The achievements of both the Army and Negro soldiers in so extensive an employment cannot be lightly dismissed."[11]

Blacks found, however, that they were ignored even if they served in combat formations and that the press wasn't interested in their exploits, no matter how gallant. One platoon sergeant with the all-black 761st Tank Battalion, which established an exemplary combat record in the ETO from November 1944 until the end of the war in May 1945, complained that white journalists would walk right past the black tankers after a battle to interview the white troops.

The reactivated 93d Division was shipped to the Pacific in World War II and, despite its limited use in combat, was generally considered to have fought well and honorably. The reactivated 92d Infantry Division saw action in Italy. As in World War I, the division's performance was questioned by the Army's hierarchy, but some observers suggest that the division's white officers were inferior leaders. It was often difficult to find white officers who wished to command black troops. Historian Lee spelled out the problems for whites:

> That few white officers would choose to serve with Negro troops became a generally accepted belief. . . . Many . . . were filled with a feeling of defeat and discouragement over their own inglorious assignments to troops whom their white associates, when they did not completely ignore their existence, were frankly skeptical.[12]

Ironically, poor performance by white combat units was often dismissed, blamed on poor leadership, or even glorified to couch the bitter reality of the defeat. Accolades for defeated white troops were never more blatant than for the fate of the 106th Division, the "Golden Lions." The division was effectively destroyed during the Battle of the Bulge when two of its three regiments surrendered wholesale during the first hours of the German attack through the Ardennes. Despite its disastrous showing, the division was eulogized in a 1946 *Saturday Evening Post* article titled "The Glorious Collapse of the 106th."

Units of the II Corps, including the 1st Infantry Division and 1st Armored Division, were defeated by Rommel's forces at the Kasserine Pass in Tunisia in 1943 during the North African campaign. Blame for that debacle was attributed to the inexperience of the troops and their commanding general, Maj. Gen. Lloyd Fredendall, who was replaced by Gen. George S. Patton.

After Kasserine, the British referred to American combat troops, all of whom were white, as "our Italians," a brutal slap at American manhood and the white infantryman. The epithet stemmed from the belief that the Tommy was as good in combat as seven Italian soldiers.

When the 1st Infantry Division, "Big Red One," went on to glory at Normandy and in the drive across Europe in 1944 and 1945, its past defeats were forgotten. Blacks were seldom given a second chance.

During the waning months of World War II in Europe, some 4,560 blacks volunteered for infantry duty. More than 2,200 were trained as infantrymen and assigned to combat units. These black volunteers were integrated into white companies by platoon rather than by individual, but it was a harbinger of the full integration in the American military that was to come within a few years. In most instances the black volunteers impressed their white comrades with their durability and bravery. It took Korea and the Vietnam War to prove finally to white Americans that African American soldiers had the same fiber as white troops.

It would be a half century before white America recognized the bravery of many of its black soldiers in World War II. In 1997, seven African American soldiers were awarded the Medal of Honor for heroism in combat during that war. Most of those medals were awarded posthumously by President Bill Clinton.

TEN

THE ODYSSEY
OF THE 514TH

The men of C Company would not ride great white stallions and wear cavalry blue. They would become truck drivers and learn the "Army way" at Fort Meade, Maryland. Driving a Jimmy was not like driving a car. There were ten gears to master, all designed to take the truck over almost any type of terrain.

This standard military vehicle was also called a six-by-six because all six groupings of wheels, two in the front and four in the rear, could be engaged at the same time when needed. The four rear duals were powered in most GMC models by two drive shafts, which gave the truck tremendous traction up hills or in the ever-present mud around supply depots in the ETO.

"You could learn to drive the truck in two or three days if you followed the instructors," James Rookard said.[1]

The most difficult aspects of driver training related to convoy operations—learning how to maintain proper speeds and intervals between trucks and to drive at night with cat eyes as the only illumination. This was dangerous work. An I Company driver was killed at Fort Meade when his truck plunged over an embankment.

C Company drivers were expected to understand carburetion and ignition and know how to change tires, check fluids, and repair most minor problems. This knowledge would be critical in the ETO, where breakdowns among Red Ball trucks became epidemic.

C Company troops went through the standard sixteen-week basic infantry training given to all World War II soldiers. The training included marksmanship with old Enfield rifles, bayonet drills, night marches, and infiltration courses where machine-gun bullets whizzed a few inches above the heads of the low-crawling troops.

Some of the men from each company of the 514th QM Truck Regiment were sent to Camp A. P. Hill, Virginia, for training with .50-caliber machine guns. Every fourth truck in a convoy was supposed to be outfitted with a machine gun ring for the .50-caliber gun that protruded out of the top of the cab, but, once at war, few trucks carried the weapon.

C Company was one of twelve companies in the 514th with unit designations from the 3901st to the 3912th. C Company was designated the 3903d. (Many trucking companies kept the QM designation even as they were being transferred to the Transportation Corps midway through the war.) Each company consisted of some 150 men and 5 white officers. All of the non-commissioned officers were black. Eventually, each company would have three platoons of sixteen trucks each.

In the summer of 1943, C Company was transferred to Camp Pickett in southern Virginia, a place where the Confederacy was not a distant memory. Pickett was located near Blackstone, not far from Appomattox Court House where Lee had surrendered his Army of Northern Virginia in 1865, and the base was named after Confederate Gen. George E. Pickett. It was not a hospitable place for blacks.

Townspeople and white soldiers made life miserable for the men in C Company. Many white troops on base were racist, and confrontations could be dangerous. "I knew better than to go into town," James Chappelle said. "I was a hothead at that time and I knew I'd probably get hurt or hurt somebody."[2] Sgt. Jack Blackwell had to hire a cab to go on leave because white soldiers would not allow him on the bus that took the troops to the train station.[3]

The summer of 1943 brought severe strain between the races on and off military bases in the country. Historian Ulysses Lee noted:

By early summer, the harvest of racial antagonism was begin-
ning to assume bumper proportions. Serious disorders
occurred at Camp Van Dorn, Mississippi; Camp Stewart,
Georgia; Lake Charles, Louisiana; March Field and Camp
San Luis Obispo, California; Fort Bliss, Texas; Camp Phillips,
Kansas; Camp Breckinridge, Kentucky; and Camp Shenango,
Pennsylvania. Other camps had lesser disorders and rumors
of unrest.

The disorders of 1943 differed from those of proceeding years.
They involved, for the most part, a larger number of troops.
They occurred more frequently in the camps themselves where
the possibility of mass conflict between men of Negro and white
units was greater. . . . Two of the disorders, those at Camps Van
Dorn and Stewart, were especially serious, both for their poten-
tialities and for their effects on the revision of plans for the
employment of Negro troops.[4]

At Camp Stewart, resentful black troops from the 264th
Infantry Regiment rampaged through a nearby town after they
heard rumors that a black woman had been raped and her husband
murdered by white troops, including white MPs. Several MPs were
wounded, and one was killed. Historian Lee reported:

> In the aftermath of the riot . . . a board of officers appointed at
> Camp Stewart to investigate determined that the disturbance
> was essentially an outgrowth of long pent-up emotions and
> resentments. The majority of the Negro soldiers were convinced
> that justice and fair treatment were not to be had by them in
> neighboring communities and that the influence of these com-
> munities was strongly reflected in the racial policies of the com-
> mand at Camp Stewart.[5]

Relief came for C Company during the winter of 1944 when
the 514th was shipped to Camp Kilmer, New Jersey, a transfer
station to the ETO. A few days later, the men boarded a ship in
New York harbor and sailed to Great Britain.

"We were all eighteen and nineteen. We didn't think we'd ever die," Chappelle recalled.[6]

"It was a wonderful feeling. We were all young and it was our first time away from home," Rookard said.[7]

"I think I was too dumb to be scared," said Herman Heard, a native Texan who had been inducted into the Army on April Fool's Day, 1943, and had joined the 514th at Fort Meade.[8]

Their ship, the former French liner *Pasteur*, had been scuttled in North Africa to prevent her from being captured by the Germans after the fall of France in 1940. She was raised by the British, repaired, and outfitted with a British crew. The cruise was a welcome respite for the men despite the fact that it was the first time at sea for most of them and, as Corporal Brice noted, despite their dislike of the English food—preserved roast beef, boiled potatoes, bitter marmalade and tea and oatmeal.

"It was strange and new to these soldier landlubbers," Brice reported. "The sea's vastness and ever-changing moods were sobering. Now, still and turquoise, later angry, gray and foaming, whipping up spray over the decks and causing the ship to dip and roll. . . ."[9]

Rumors were rife. Brice noted that there were reports one night that the *Pasteur* had had a brush with a German submarine and that the ship slowed to "let a whole fleet of U-boats go by." There was also the persistent rumor, more a prayer, that the war would be over before the *Pasteur* arrived in port.

Life on board ship was pleasant. The men attended movies and amateur theatrical productions and lost themselves in books and magazines. "In the evening, when open decks were cleared, the favorite pastime of many, was to stroll around the enclosed 'B' deck. Some of the boys formed impromptu vocal groups and gravitated to their chosen spot on the deck each evening to hold forth," Brice wrote.[10]

After nine days, the coast of Ireland appeared in the early dawn, and the men crowded the decks to glimpse this new land as the *Pasteur* continued through the Irish Sea and past the coast of Scotland and the Isle of Man. A Royal Air Force (RAF) aircraft swooped over at mast height and dipped its wings in salute as the ship approached port. The *Pasteur* arrived in Liverpool later that day, and tugs escorted the liner into the harbor— past waving onlookers welcoming the Yanks and past the first signs of war, a Liberty ship near the harbor entrance that had been cut in two.

England was seething with preparations for the invasion of France. More than a million American troops were stationed at bases and bivouac areas throughout the kingdom, many of them in isolated villages on the south coast. By D-Day, the strength of American forces in Great Britain numbered more than 1,527,000. To maintain this massive fighting force, more than 5 million long tons of supplies had been landed. The men of the 514th immediately went to work as they hauled materiel from depots to ports and from ports to depots.

C Company's first bivouac was at Martock, a village in Somerset. The company later moved to Piddletrenthide, not far from the channel coast in Dorset, which was known for its yellowstone houses scattered along the base of the Piddle Valley. The men were surrounded by ancient houses, and a gargoyled fifteenth-century church was at the northern end of the village. There were wonderful views of the Dorset countryside, and there were pubs and women—white women.

I Company was encamped at Biddulph in Straffordshire near the River Trent and the Bridestones, a Neolithic burial chamber where, legend says, a Viking warrior and his English bride are buried. This was strange stuff for these soldiers from the New World.

If the men believed life would be better in racially tolerant Great Britain, many were quickly disillusioned. In retrospect, some from C Company felt that the racial climate in England was the worst that they experienced during the war, with the exception, for some members, of the time spent at Camp Pickett.

C Company veterans explain this paradox by noting that, although the British citizens were, for the most part, racially tolerant, the American Army, which had the ultimate authority over them, was not. If anything, racisim became more virulent. The British often found the blacks to be more mannerly and polite than American whites and were appalled by their treatment in the U.S. Army. There were few black British citizens, and the nation had never developed the raw prejudices and policies of segregation as had Americans. Rather than objects of hate and derision, American blacks were regarded with fascination and, to many racist Americans, this was even more reason to be intolerant of black U.S. troops.

One thirteen-year-old British girl's first encounter with black American troops was described by Norman Longmate in his book, *The G.I.s: The Americans in Britain, 1942–1945*:

> Huge vehicles dominated the lanes and quickly all of us children were off to investigate. The only dark Americans I had seen were on films or in history books, so it was shattering and fascinating to see not one darkie soldier but hundreds. . . . The thing which stood out most were the palms of their hands . . . almost pink, the sparkling white teeth and glinting eyes against the dark skin, the gentleness and big stature.
>
> They quickly made friends and we were happy to sit and listen. We didn't need story books, here were people of a strange land, speaking a different kind of English, a different colour; this was a storybook come to life. Colour prejudice just didn't happen. We learnt they were just like us underneath, same joys, fears, love and feelings.[11]

The men of I Company were welcomed by the people of Biddulph. "We were invited everywhere; and considerable effort was made to keep us entertained. The facilities of practically every organization that could be of service, was made available to us," Corporal Brice recorded. The Central Methodist Church established a canteen, and the British Women's Volunteer Service provided a game room with table tennis, darts, a piano, radios, and magazines.[12]

British girls found nothing objectionable about dating black men, and Brice listed some of the activities:

> Almost nightly dances were held and the girls came from all of the neighboring towns to attend them. Sometimes the 514th Band Group would play and things would really get gay in response to their torrid rhythms and harmonies. Things would really jump and the jitterbugging would do justice to Harlem's home of happy feet, the Savoy.[13]

But trouble was brewing. To whites raised in prewar America, the concept of black men with free will and free to date and become sexually involved with white English women was anathema. "A bunch of us went to the social and it didn't take very long—some of them were wandering out the door with white girls and going off into the bushes and I'll never forget it," said a white officer who attended a church gathering in Salisbury with members of his all-black unit. "I turned to this Englishman and asked if he approved of his young women going out into the bushes with blacks and so forth. He said, 'Oh yes, we have no racial distinctions over here.' "[14]

"If you were lucky enough to get a white lady, so be it," Rookard said. "All the guys were doing it. African Americans had to have women. They were away from home. But the white Americans couldn't stand for an African American to be with a white lady. They were just that way."[15]

In September 1942, General Eisenhower described the British attitude toward race relations in a letter to Maj. Gen. Alexander D. Surles, Chief of the War Department's Public Relations Branch:

> Here we have a very thickly populated country that is devoid of racial consciousness. They know nothing at all about the conventions and habits that have been developed in the U.S. in order to preserve a segregation in social activity. . . . To most British people, including the village girls—even those of

perfectly fine character—the Negro soldier is just another man, rather fascinating because he is unique in their experience, a jolly fellow and with money to spend. Our own white soldiers, seeing a girl walk down the street with a Negro, frequently see themselves as protectors of the weaker sex and believe it necessary to intervene even to the extent of using force, to let her know what she's doing.[16]

Nonetheless, Eisenhower issued orders that an official policy of segregation of social activities by American forces in Britain would not be tolerated. But trying to do away with centuries of prejudice could not be accomplished with the stroke of a pen.

Many blacks were angered that white soldiers were trying to convince British children that blacks were part monkey and had tails. "The Caucasian Americans were telling this to the British," Rookard remembered. "One time I got out of my truck and this little girl came up to me and starting walking around me and she kept looking. I said 'What's the matter,' and she said 'I don't see it.' I said, 'Well what are you looking for?' She said 'I don't see your tail.' That's the way they were, the Caucasians."[17]

Stories of white prejudice and criminal behavior against blacks were legion. "Hell, you know that every time black and white soldiers got together there would be a fight," Chappelle said. In Newton Abbot in Devon there were so many fights between white and black troops that the town restricted the two races to different nights on the town.

Black troops often were permitted into towns and villages only when accompanied by one of their officers. Even then, the blacks frequently were accompanied by "snowdrops" (MPs), who were present to ensure that whites and blacks did not mingle. "There had to be one officer and one snowdrop every time they [blacks] went on pass. If you had more than ten men you took two MPs," said one white officer in a black unit. "You'd drop the men off and check in with the local police station to tell them where you were, how many men were in town and then we could do what we wanted. But we usually stayed with the men."[18]

One night, Charles Stevenson barely succeeded in dissuading a group of his black troops from arming themselves and returning to Plymouth to seek revenge against white sailors with whom they had fought earlier in the evening:

> I heard a lot of noise in our arms tent and went in there and there's about ten or twelve of my guys, some of them half-tanked. "We're goin' down there and clean those whitey sons-of-bitches out," they all said. I talked to them for half an hour and talked them out of it and made sure the arms stayed locked and put a guard on the rifles. We went downtown and reported the incident to the MPs, and they went looking for these white guys, but this was just before the invasion and the town was filled with sailors and ships.[19]

Lt. William A. Harnist interceded one night when groups of whites and blacks confronted each other in a parking lot outside Salisbury after one of the blacks had allegedly knifed a white soldier. The white troops were southerners and taunted the blacks with slurs. Officers and MPs were finally able to control the situation.[20]

Racial taunts were commonplace. One time, for instance, as black truck drivers hauled white airborne troops during maneuvers in England prior to the invasion, they were ridiculed by the paratroopers with racial epithets. But the blacks had the last word. Instead of keeping intervals between trucks at the required distance, the drivers closed up to within a few feet of each other. Dust from the dirt road blew up behind each truck and was sucked into the covered truck bed where the paratroops were seated. By the time the trip was over, the paratroopers were a coughing, speechless, and filthy lot.

Despite the problems of race, the business of war was paramount. "We drove troops to the coast constantly on dry runs," Chappelle said. "We'd take them up and bring them back." On several occasions, C Company was involved in practice landings with infantrymen who would soon be landing at Normandy.[21]

By spring, the preinvasion activity on the south coast was frenzied. I Company received new trucks, as well as rifles, ammunition, grenades, and even bazookas. The coastal counties of Cornwall, Devon, and Dorset were filled with American troops. The 29th Division was training in Cornwall, and the 4th Division, which would land at Utah Beach, was training on Bodman moor in Devon. The harbors were crowded with ships of the invasion fleet. The evenings were sometimes filled with the roar of German planes seeking targets along these coastal enclaves that, during the weeks before the invasion, had been sealed off from outside view.

Security was so strict that, in some cases, drivers were not told of their destinations or the types of supplies they were carrying to embarkation points. The commanding officer of one of C Company's sister units was not informed about one of his platoons' missions to the south coast; he was told only after his company had landed in France.

It was no secret to the men of the 514th that their destination was France. D-Day had put them on notice. A few days following the invasion, C Company's trucks were waterproofed for the ride out of the surf at Utah Beach. Waterproofing entailed packing spark plugs, distributors, and electrical system connections with a puttylike substance. The air cleaner was removed, and a flexible hose was attached to the carburetor, run out of the engine compartment, and fastened to the windshield. Hosing also was attached to the exhaust pipe and extended up the side of the truck to a point well above any water line. Drivers stripped to their underwear and drove the trucks into large 6-foot–deep pits filled with water to test the waterproofing.

I Company pulled out of Biddulph and headed for Southampton in preparation for assignment to France. The men were forbidden any contact with civilians. British currency was collected and an invasion currency of French francs issued. Each soldier was given a packet of necessities that included a booklet of French phrases and words, information about France and the

French, D-ration chocolate, cigarettes, seasick pills, and a vomit bag for the trip across the channel.

The unit drove through the suburbs of Southampton to a pier where it would depart for France. Corporal Brice reported the events in his history:

> The men on the whole were quiet on this early morning trip to the pier, apparently in deep thought. The way led through prosperous and well kept residential suburbs of Southampton. Beautifully landscaped grounds were all around us, tall stately trees lined the walks and the war seemed as remote as if we were in an American suburb.
>
> Soon we approached the business section and the contrast was startling. . . . Shells of buildings, long irregular bare spaces that wound for blocks where buildings had been, came into view, all park areas were converted into air raid shelters, barbed wire barricades were up. It sent shivers down my spine to think of the fiery caldron this area must have been at some time past with fire bombs and high explosives raining down from overhead. "We knew we were ready for business."[22]

ELEVEN

EFFECTIVE CHAOS

The Red Ball Express was a seat-of-the-pants operation, organized in extreme haste, with frequent administrative and operational breakdowns. Problems were most apparent at the beginning but continued throughout its existence. Truck drivers often avoided the Red Ball Highway to take side roads, bypassed regulating stations, ignored speed limits and maintenance, and cursed at MPs who tried to bring them in line. "The newly formed Red Ball organization clinked and clattered, groaned and wheezed," noted one G-4 history.[1] And it got the job done.

MTB officers immediately established traffic-control points (TCPs) that operated around the clock at principal intersections and in towns. The job of TCP personnel was to regulate convoys or any other vehicles, civilian or military, that used the dedicated highway and to ensure that Red Ball convoys had the right-of-way in all cases. TCP troops kept daily records of the arrival times of passing convoys and logged their destinations, weights, and the classes of supplies that they carried. TCP personnel also were required to have maps of alternate routes for non–Red Ball vehicles, as well as maps of the Red Ball route that showed the location of refueling points and maintenance shops for legitimate convoys and vehicles.

So much for the plans. When Chartres-bound convoys from the 3630th QM Truck Company passed through the TCP at Saint-Lô on Red Ball's inaugural day, no maps were available. The convoy leader found his way by asking directions from American troops encountered along the way and by referring to a *Stars and Stripes* map that showed the location of the front lines.[2]

This was a typical experience on the recently opened Red Ball. Few drivers knew the Red Ball route. Many convoys made their way toward the forward depots on dead reckoning as they passed through towns that would soon be well established destination points on the Red Ball: Vire, Flers, Argentan, L'Aigle, Verneuil, Châteauneauf-en-Thymerais, and, finally, Chartres.

Perplexed officers tried to learn why convoys were avoiding the Red Ball Highway and found that their orders did not specify that the trucks were expected to stay on the dedicated route: "Their orders read: 'Go to Chartres'—'Deliver this to FUSA [First U.S. Army]. Many drivers who had set out alone did not even know the Red Ball route existed."[3] Even some high-ranking officers were unaware of the Red Ball's existence in its early days. The G-4 history noted:

> Perhaps the "fog of battle" hung over the rear area as well as the combat zone. At any rate, even AdSec's [Advanced Section of COMZ] G-4 didn't know until the afternoon of 27 August what the full Red Ball route was. First reports reaching him caused TCP personnel to be placed at Verneuil on Route N 24, where they waited three days for trucks to come along consigned to Third Army. None came, and only 7 vehicles for First Army. The trucks were getting through somehow, but by other routes.[4]

TCPs also were supposed to double as rest areas where trucks refueled, minor repairs were made, and drivers received instructions and enjoyed hot coffee and sandwiches. But these services were going unused as the trucks found other routes to their destinations. TCPs had been established at Saint-Lô, Vire, Domfront, Alençon, Mortagne-au-Perche, La Loupe, Chartres, Nogent-le-Rotrou, Bellême, Mamers, Villaines-la-Juhel, Mayenne, and Mortain.

The Army also established regulating stations that directed trucks to the proper depots and notified depot personnel when convoys were to arrive.[5] These units were also being bypassed and were not receiving advance notice of approaching convoys in order to inform the dumps when to be ready for the trucks. The 25th Regulating Station improvised by sending messengers hurrying to the depots after a convoy passed by, which gave depot personnel at least a few minutes' warning.

Maintenance patrols also were conspicuously absent from long stretches of the Red Ball Highway even into the middle of September. The G-4 history of the Red Ball noted:

> Since 10 September no highway patrols has [sic] been found between Mortagne and Chartres and the Seine River.
>
> The 27 companies of the 27th QM Group (TC) had no maintenance between 10 and 12 September. This group patrolled the return route from Chartres to St. Lô.
>
> No Ordnance service could be located at the St. Cyr diversion point on 10 and 11 September, and no patrols passed the point where the Red Ball route divided into First and Third Army routes. A special search, without result, was made for maintenance patrols to meet 15 specific requests for assistance, one of which involved 8 vehicles or a battery of 155-mm guns. This battery passed the St. Cyr point three times looking for help.
>
> Requests for assistance and locations of maintenance facilities were received continually from Group, Battalion and Company commanders. A definite search for five hours on 15 September found no maintenance installations or road patrols, but did disclose vehicles which had been lying along the road, unserviceable for three to five days.[6]

Adding to the difficulties was a shortage of tow trucks. Many Jimmies were left stranded on road shoulders for days before they were towed to a repair shop. On 10 September, a spot check on one section of the Red Ball showed eighty-one loaded vehicles sitting unserviced along the highway between Vire and Dreux. Outside Versailles, where the Red Ball split north and south, another report indicated that as many as fifteen calls for maintenance assistance went unanswered. One of the calls came from an artillery battery making its way to the front. There were so many broken-down trucks that, on some parts of the Red Ball, the Army turned to Piper Cub airplanes to report their locations to repair units.[7]

Each heavy automotive maintenance company working on the highway had two 4-ton and two 10-ton wreckers, and the medium automotive maintenance units had two 4-ton wreckers, but this was insufficient capacity to handle all of the disabled vehicles. It became necessary to assign fifty 4-ton Diamond-Ts to wrecker duties to solve the salvage problem on the Red Ball.[8]

Efficiency also suffered because of divided responsibilities and control. The Red Ball passed through several base sections (separate COMZ administrative zones), each under separate command and each with its own regulations governing the highway. In one case, COMZ established procedure for Red Ball shipments in the Normandy Base Section, but neglected to issue the same orders to the Loire Section commander even though Red Ball was operating through Loire at that time. Also, these same orders did not apply to the Seine and Oise Sections when Red Ball entered those areas.[9] Red Ball trucks also were being diverted to rail transfer points without authorization from the proper commanders.[10]

Traffic control was a major problem on the Red Ball, and MPs did the best they could to ride herd on the convoys. The 804th MP Company learned how difficult it was to deal with a driver whose sole objective was to get his cargo to the front as fast as possible:

If directed one way GIs had a tendency to go the other way. . . . When the American soldier told the MP where he (the MP) could go, and where he (the driver) intended to go, it wasn't out of orneriness. It was due rather to the GI's determination to carry out the dicta of General Forrest [Civil War general] relevant to getting there "fustest with the mostest." And so, many a time, the man on post had to cuss the GI, while blessing him in his heart. In the words of one of our men, "the American soldier has the habit of going straight at his objective." It was this habit which won the war.[11]

The job of the MPs in traffic control on the Red Ball was critical to the success of the operation. There were thousands of vehicles on the highway, all in a hurry and all expecting priority treatment, but there were never enough MPs and those assigned to the Red Ball had too many other responsibilities. In September, the 804th was assigned to the Red Ball in Soissons some 30 miles northeast of Paris. The MPs' duties, however, went well beyond traffic control. They included guarding a large cache of food left behind by the retreating Germans, removal of two snipers in a church steeple who were harassing the town, and the management of a steady stream of German prisoners flowing back from the front, including one batch of ten thousand POWs from the disintegrating German Seventh Army.

There were hundreds of miles of Red Ball Highway to patrol, intersections to manage, detours to point out, and bridges to guard. The Army recognized the severity of the MP shortage. On 1 September, Col. Hugh H. Tolman, commander of the 513th QM Truck Regiment, noted in a meeting with his unit commanders:

> You have a Major General, who is Provost Marshall of ASCZ [Advanced Section Communications Zone] doing everything possible that they can to eliminate other traffic from the road and helping to direct our own traffic. I think it is getting a little better. I know Ordnance Service is not sufficient. I know that Military Police Service is not sufficient, but we are doing the best we can, but everybody must put his shoulder to the wheel and try to correct these things.[12]

Colonel Tolman urged his officers to take men from the trucking companies for police patrol duty on the Red Ball Highway and in the towns:

> The Military Police do not have sufficient personnel to patrol the highways of the Red Ball Route. I can advise the CG [commanding general] of the situation, and I'm sure that he will take action to get additional MP's. This is the most important job that there is going on, other than penetrating Germany, at this time, according to him. I am sure that the officers are doing everything they can to correct the situation, but there are just not enough men to do . . . anything else except to try to regulate the traffic.[13]

In a letter of 21 September, Gen. John C. H. Lee, COMZ commander, exhorted all MP units to pursue their duties:

> You don't have to be told that the Army moves on wheels. And just as the human body needs an unimpaired circulation to keep alive, the vital force that gives our fighting forces its Sunday punch is your Red Ball Route. You are a guardian of that all-important highway. It's your job to insure that the critically needed supplies that roll past your post flow in a smooth, uninterrupted stream towards the front.[14]

Lee spelled out the rules that he expected to be enforced on the Red Ball route:

> 1) KEEP INTERSECTIONS CLEAR—Remove broken-down vehicles by towing if necessary.
> 2) KEEP ALL CIVILIAN TRAFFIC OFF THE ROUTE—Unless authorized in writing by an MP officer.
> 3) KEEP CIVILIANS OFF OUR VEHICLES. Report all violations.
> 4) DO NOT PERMIT CONVOYS TO BE SPLIT AT INTERSECTIONS.

5) DO NOT PERMIT RED BALL TRUCKS TO LEAVE THE ROUTE—Unless authorized to do so in writing.

6) KNOW BY HEART ALL THE HIGHWAYS IN YOUR AREA. It will help keep the convoys from going astray.

7) AT NIGHT USE YOUR LIGHT SIGNALS PROPERLY. Remember you can see the truck easier than the driver can see you. Your mission is an important one. Give it all you've got and the war will be over that much sooner.[15]

It is surprising that the Red Ball was not plagued with even greater chaos during its early days. There was no precedent for such a large-scale motorized supply operation. In England before the invasion, the Army had considered but never tested a long-haul supply line, similar to Red Ball, that would use tractor-trailer combinations over long stretches of highway. This would have provided a dry rehearsal that might have alleviated some of Red Ball's problems in advance.

The difficulties on the Red Ball prompted the Army to establish more comprehensive rules and regulations, but the new regulations were not issued until 2 December, nearly a month after Red Ball was discontinued.[16] Although they were issued too late to help the Red Ball, they streamlined the later trucking lines that operated as American forces pushed into Germany in March 1945.

The irony of the Red Ball is that it achieved its greatest successes during the chaotic first weeks of operation. The Transportation Corps' original projections were to transport 75,000 tons of supplies, excluding bulk POL, to the Chartres-La Loupe-Dreux area by 1 September. The 75,000-ton target was exceeded when Red Ball trucks carried 88,939 tons through 5 September.[17]

The tonnages included 15,040 tons, Class I supplies—rations; 27,232 tons, Class II supplies—clothing and weapons; 19,047 tons, Class III supplies—POL; 2,559 tons, Class IV supplies—construction material; and 25,061 tons, Class V supplies—ammunition.[18]

The newly formed Red Ball organization somehow managed to get the job done. Although the GIs might have described it this way: "Situation normal, all f----- up," the Army had the last word in its later reports on the operation, "It rolled. It got the goods where they were wanted." But the Army also admitted this was accomplished "largely by the grace of God."[19]

TWELVE

ACROSS THE SEINE

The Red Ball and the American armies drove on. In late August, it seemed as though the war would soon be over, and, for some, the fighting turned glorious as described by one of Patton's officers:

> There was blood and death every hour during those mellow August days in the heart of France. But life was also gusty and exciting and fast-moving. There were great deeds of daring, skill, and endurance, breath-taking breakthrough, and slashing envelopments. Above all, there was vaulting esprit. Cockily, Third Army men were confident nothing could stop them; that soon they would "run out of France" and be racing through Germany to final victory.[1]

Hodges's First Army also advanced on the Reich. It did not stop until its lead elements nearly reached Aachen, Germany. By 2 September, General Bradley believed that the Germans were so badly mauled "that with an all-out effort we could crack through the Siegfried Line, reach the Rhine and establish beachheads on the east bank within a week." Bradley urged his commanders to "exploit the collapse with everything at our disposal without stopping for supplies—pursuit without pause."[2]

Bradley's plan was a two-pronged thrust north and south of the Ardennes. The objective of the northern thrust was to span the Rhine River after a drive due east from Brussels through Liège (Belgium) and Aachen to Cologne (Germany). It would be undertaken by three corps of Hodges's First Army—Lt. Gen. B. G. Horrocks's XXX, Maj. Gen. Charles Corlett's XIX, and Maj. Gen. Lawton Collins's VII.

The southern thrust, led by Patton's Third Army, would jump off from the Meuse River bridgeheads and drive directly east to the Rhine through the Saar toward Frankfurt, Germany. It would consist of three corps, Maj. Gen. Walton Walker's XX, Maj. Gen. Manton Eddy's XII, and Maj. Gen. Wade Haislip's XV.

Augmenting both thrusts would be Maj. Gen. Leonard T. Gerow's V Corps, which would swing south of the Ardennes and Luxembourg to fill the gap between Patton and Hodges. Maj. Gen. Troy Middleton's VIII Corps, besieging the ports in Brittany, was relieved by the newly formed Ninth Army and free to join Bradley's anticipated push into Germany.[3]

Bradley noted that Eisenhower approved his plan but with reservations. "Ike was concerned that owing to the logistical crisis we might be attempting too much too soon."[4] The supreme commander was right. But had Eisenhower not ordered his armies over the Seine while waiting for an improved logistical system, he would have been condemned for not attempting a knockout blow against Hitler in 1944.

As the armies moved east toward the German frontier, the Red Ball was extended beyond Paris into eastern France in the second and longest phase of the operation. Instead of creating one large loop route similar to that from Normandy to the Chartres area, the Red Ball beyond Paris established two new loop routes that branched north and south to serve an ever-expanding front that stretched from Belgium nearly to the Swiss border.

On the flatlands of eastern France, the Red Ball roared on as rapidly as before. "Still maintaining the bridge here in Melun," Sergeant Giles wrote on 6 September 1944. "Main Red Ball highway goes through here. Believe me, these boys are in a hurry & if you don't get out of the way fast they'd just as soon knock you over as not. Well it's getting to be a long haul from the beaches of Normandy to the front & they have to get in a hell of hurry to keep the stuff moving."[5]

Drivers on the northern leg of Red Ball skirted Paris and passed through the industrial suburb of Saint-Denis as they headed northeast toward Soissons. The north fork of the new highway followed Route 2 through Villers-Cotterêts before reaching Soissons 30 miles northeast of Paris. On its return leg, it ran south from Soissons to Château-Thierry, Coulommiers to Fontainebleau, and back to Chartres.

The southern leg of the extended Red Ball Highway ran southeasterly to Melun, Fontenay-Trésigny, and Rozay-en-Brie, then east on Route 4 to Esternay and Sommesous. The trucks ran through wide open space that, in the dwindling days of summer and in the early fall, was a vast, verdant plain dotted here and there with compact villages.

The return route on the southern fork ran back through Arcis-sur-Aube and Nogent-sur-Seine and also back to Fontainebleau and Chartres. Trucks on the northern route carried supplies to the First Army. Red Ball traffic on the southern leg supplied elements of the First Army and all of Patton's Third Army.

The rumbling Jimmies soon bypassed Soissons and Arcis-sur-Aube. As the front moved into Belgium and toward the German frontier, drivers on the northern leg of the Red Ball were traveling to Hirson, France, on the Belgian frontier. On the southern leg, they were going all the way to Verdun and Metz.

With the extension of the Red Ball into eastern France, the length of the highway had nearly tripled. To reach Metz, trucks traveled more than 200 miles from the Paris area, or about the same distance as from Saint-Lô to Chartres. The trip from Paris to Hirson was about 130 miles. The total roundtrip length of the Red Ball Highway from Normandy to Belgium was now some 686 miles on the northern route and 590 on the southern route.

Adding to the length of the highway was the fact that Red Ball drivers entered a kind of no-man's-land near the front, where they often drove in search of a supply depot. They would be told that a depot was at one spot only to find that it had moved on, and the truckers lost valuable time in search of a place to unload. These extended trips sometimes added 50 miles to a journey.

Although Hirson and Verdun were the official termination points of the Red Ball, trucks and convoys often drove beyond them. By early September, the First Army had advanced well into Belgium and was preparing for the assault into Germany near Aachen. Red Ball trucks frequently drove through to Liège, where a massive supply base was being developed.

When Red Ball trucks first entered Belgium, the drivers often did not know whether they were in German or Allied territory. On one night run to the front, two truckers from the 146th were routed through Brussels. Fearing that the Germans still controlled the city, the drivers sped through the dark, deserted streets at such breakneck speeds that they occasionally side-swiped buildings.[6]

To the south, Red Ball trucks converged on Verdun where another large supply depot was being established to support the Third Army's advance into Germany. I Company moved to this World War I battlefield in mid-September. Corporal Brice described the site in his history:

> Verdun is geographically striking. High hills surround it, and without any knowledge of the requirements of a strategic position, you get the impression that this is one. Old grass covered trenches honeycomb the hills and area beyond. Along the southern side of the city we passed the newly constructed "Eagle Airstrip." C-47s, P-47s and Piper Cubs were landing and taking off in quick succession.[7]

The Verdun and Liège dumps were strategically positioned by Bradley's 12th Army Group to supply the eventual drive into Germany. Liège was located behind the First Army's left flank, and Verdun was behind its right flank, so both could meet the needs of the First and Third Armies. Both depots also supported two new American armies created in the fall of 1944, the Ninth under Lt. Gen. William H. Simpson and the Fifteenth under Major General Gerow.

In the final assault on Germany in 1945, Bradley was able to draw more heavily from the Liège dumps for the envelopment of the Ruhr Valley and then shift to the Verdun depots as Patton's forces wheeled into southern Germany. Backing up Liège and Verdun was the 62d QM Base Depot at Charleroi, Belgium.[8] The value of all three bases was seen even before the final advance into Germany, when they supplied American troops during the Battle of the Bulge.

Red Ball units were put to the test in early September when Field Marshal Montgomery's 21st Army group faced a transport crisis of potentially catastrophic proportions. Some 1,400 new British trucks were out of action because of faulty engines, and the problem was compounded when an accompanying shipment of spare engines was also found to be defective. These trucks were to have been used to supply Operation Market Garden, the airborne and land invasion of Holland to establish a bridgehead on the east bank of the Rhine. Montgomery believed that if he achieved this objective, his armies could make a dash for Berlin and end the war in 1944.[9]

The job of supplying Market Garden fell to the Americans, and Eisenhower ordered the daily transport of some 500 tons of supplies from Bayeux, in the Normandy base area, to Brussels. This put an additional burden on the Red Ball at a time when there was a critical shortage of trucks, and COMZ began scouring units throughout the American forces in the ETO for nonessential vehicles. Vehicles and drivers were requisitioned from evacuation hospitals, gas treatment battalions, mobile refrigerator companies, salvage and repair companies, engineer camouflage units, signal depot and repair companies, and ordnance maintenance units. Ten trucking companies consisting of some 340 vehicles came from antiaircraft units that had seen little action because of the Luftwaffe's decline. In the Normandy base section, two engineer general service regiments were each reorganized into seven truck companies and a chemical smoke-generating battalion was fashioned into four trucking companies.

The largest number of trucks and drivers came from idled U.S. infantry divisions awaiting transfer to the front. Forty companies of 1,500 trucks were pulled from three divisions bivouacked in Normandy. Initially, these units included the 26th, 95th, and 104th Divisions, but trucks and drivers also came from the 102d, 94th, and 84th Divisions. Newly arrived combat divisions were held in reserve for several weeks in rear areas because the lack of supplies made it impossible to equip and provision them adequately at the front. Just transporting the troops of an entire division forward also would have required streams of Jimmies driving back and forth day and night.

In all, the U.S. Army created some sixty-one provisional truck companies whose service was invaluable. According to Ruppenthal:

> There is no doubt that but for these special measures in marshaling the transportation resources in both the communications and combat zones the advance of the armies could not have been sustained as far as it was. Throughout the period of the pursuit, motor transport, contrary to all expectations, bore the preponderant burden of supply movement over distances up to 400 miles.[10]

THIRTEEN

NEVER VOLUNTEER

Thousands of white infantrymen were pouring into France during the late summer of 1944. Before going into the lines, these men faced weeks in muddy, rain-swept bivouacs in Normandy, where they trained incessantly and waited to "marry up" with their equipment.

There was an alternative for some of these troops, for a few weeks at least. The Army needed drivers for the Red Ball Express and asked for volunteers. Despite the old Army adage, "Never volunteer," infantrymen signed up by the hundreds. Life on the Red Ball had to be better than existence in the camps.

Philo Rockwell King III, an artilleryman with the newly arrived 102d Division, answered the call for drivers:

> After we had been bivouacked in the hedgerows of Normandy, trying to buy "Calvados" [apple brandy] from any passing Frenchman, sleeping and standing guard in the rain for two or three weeks, the call came down for truck drivers. Most of the drivers attached to the unit were required to volunteer, but for the rest of us, it was anyone who thought he could drive. Most of the men knew enough not to volunteer for anything at all, but this seemed like a great chance to see the countryside and get the hell away from the unit, and especially the First Sergeant.[1]

Phillip Dick was happy to volunteer. He explained, "It was miserable and muddy in the division camps. About one hundred guys volunteered and twenty were left behind and they were furious."[2]

Like most of the volunteers, Dick had never driven a truck, and the Army had to teach him how to handle a Jimmy.

> They took us to a depot loaded with trucks. It was pitch black and nobody had any flashlights. They said "everybody get into a truck. . . ." I was supposed to turn a knob to start the vehicle but I couldn't find it. I couldn't even find where the brake handle was.[3]

Some knobs and levers were complete mysteries. On the right of the floor-mounted gear shift were two smaller levers that resembled gear shifts. The one to the right engaged the front wheel drive. The one on the left gave the vehicle an extra-low range in all gears. The driver had to learn how to use them all. Dick was at a loss:

> A fellow came along and started the truck for me and said, "OK, you're on your own." Everybody was stripping gears all the way during our first lesson. You had to learn how to double-clutch and when to shift into different gears. But by the time we got back that night we could all make the trucks go.[4]

Double-clutching was an important element of driving a 2½-ton truck. The driver had to learn to use the clutch as he took the truck out of one gear and to pump the clutch again before going into the next gear. The purpose of double-clutching was to get all components in the engine and transmission spinning at the same speed. Modern technology has made double-clutching largely unnecessary.

Merle Gutherie, also with the 102d Division, learned quickly. "When you watch somebody long enough you can do anything, particularly when it's necessary. I was young and figured I could do it."[5]

After the first few days, these "provisionals" were as proficient at driving as were the regulars, and they soon encountered the same problems of driving endlessly without sleep and steering through winding, narrow village streets. As the convoys approached the German frontier, fear lurked around every bend in the road and in the sky where the remnants of the Luftwaffe were occasionally on the prowl.

Dick's unit was stationed in a safe area near the village of Houdan about halfway to Paris from Saint-Lô on the first leg of the Red Ball Highway. Convoys set out from the village, via the northern leg of the highway, for the Normandy depots to pick up supplies and returned to Houdan on the southern leg. The roundtrip took about twenty-four hours. A second team of drivers transported the loaded trucks to the Paris area and then returned to Houdan. "We had one set of trucks and two sets of drivers," Dick said. He added that the men enjoyed the trips to Normandy, where hard cider and Calvados awaited them at the end of the day. "We went through every single village along the route. The roads were so narrow and when we got to the towns you could only go about 10 mph." Dick said. "That's why there was one-way traffic."[6]

Civilian and nonauthorized traffic sometimes illegally used the Red Ball Highway. Dick remembered a small French car sneaking onto the highway and trying to pass his convoy. To do that on the Red Ball was a test of driving skills because the trucks stuck to the center of the highway to avoid the shoulders, and the car had to weave between the vehicles. As the driver pulled in between two Jimmies, the convoy halted and the car was smashed between two trucks.

Dick became a convoy navigator riding in the lead jeep or truck. "I think they figured scout corporals should be able to find the right roads." He was issued maps, but they lacked detail so Dick memorized route numbers and place names and set out, often blind.[7] Many navigators became lost, particularly during the early days of the Red Ball when there were few traffic-directing MPs or road signs.

John Rearigh, an artilleryman with the 283d Field Artillery Battalion, who drove on the Red Ball from 10 September until 6 October, set out in a Jimmy stacked to the top of the cargo bed with artillery shells. "That was a lot of weight, but those trucks were built to handle that heavy load." To the drivers it may have appeared that way; to the maintenance men who later serviced the trucks, the excessive loads were ruinous to suspensions, engines, transmissions and tires. Rearigh's provisional trucking outfit made frequent trips to the growing depot area around Liège. "We drove in convoys about 60 miles each way along roads lined with trees on both sides. There was no officer, just enlisted men, and we maintained speeds of about 40 mph, mainly during the day."[8]

"I drove all night, or most of it, and fell asleep many times. I once was awakened as the truck left the road," said volunteer driver Fred Schlunz, an infantryman with the 102d Division. Resley Hibshman, a driver pulled from the 379th Field Artillery Battalion, 102d Division, survived one stint behind the wheel that lasted seventy-two hours without rest. "We got back to the outfit for eight hours to wash, shave, get a good meal, a wink of sleep, and we were off again," Hibshman said.[9]

In an effort to keep the trucks rolling, many Jimmies returned empty from the forward depots rather than wait long hours to be reloaded. Other trucks, however, were loaded with the aftermath of war, including expended shell casings, empty jerricans, German POWs, and, sometimes the most grisly cargo of all, the dead—silent, motionless, bloodied, and wrapped in mattress covers. Driver Kenneth Duncan will never forget hauling corpses:

> The bad part was the odor—you couldn't get the smell out of the truck. By the time you got them back and unloaded them there'd be like a black jell stringing out of the truck bed and hanging through the cracks in the floorboards. You couldn't hardly wash it off.[10]

Many a Red Ball veteran recalled seeing endless streams of Jimmies bringing the dead back to the military cemeteries in Normandy. As the fighting moved across France and into the Low Countries, the trucks transported the dead to cemeteries in eastern France and in Belgium, Luxembourg, and Holland. American soldiers killed overseas during World War II were buried in temporary cemeteries near the areas where they fell. Only after the war were they returned to the States if their families desired that they be sent home.

The Army liked the provisionals because they were often better disciplined than the regular Red Ball drivers. One provisional remembered the cowboying regulars, "Some of those guys would try and spoil our convoys. They would try to split us up. They'd be driving along and try to cut in. Maybe it was because we were white and they were black. . . . "[11]

Nevertheless, the veteran recollected with a laugh, "We also drove kind of crazy."[12]

FOURTEEN

RED BALL TRUCKS DON'T BRAKE

Stop that son of a bitch!"

Pfc. William Coursey floored the jeep and took off after a solitary Jimmy speeding down the Red Ball route east of Paris at more than 50 mph. An artilleryman with the 102d Infantry Division, Coursey had volunteered for duty on the Red Ball. As the colonel's driver, he and the colonel were a self-appointed detail to stop speeding trucks. Few vehicles stayed within the 25-mph speed limit set by the Army. Most were doing 40 mph or more, and many were pushing 60 mph. The colonel and Coursey wore themselves out patrolling the Red Ball Highway.

Coursey came alongside the truck and signaled the driver to pull over. The colonel slid from his seat and barged up to the truck cab where the driver nervously waited.

"You know the speed limit on this highway is 25 mph."

"Yes, sir."

"Well, what have you got to say for yourself, soldier?"

The driver stammered at the sight of a bird colonel. "Sir, I'm tryin' to catch up with the other guys."

"You stay in the speed limit, soldier. That's an order."

"Yes, sir!"

The colonel walked authoritatively back to the jeep. Coursey threw the vehicle in gear and shot off down the highway after more violators. Ten miles down the road, he pulled the jeep to the side and waited. Another truck, traveling at a high rate of speed, soon came into view. Within minutes, the truck was identifiable. It was the same Jimmy that they had pulled over minutes before. The colonel waved off Coursey to tell him not to pursue.

"I ought to court-martial that bastard," the colonel growled.[1]

It wouldn't have done much good. There was a saying: "Red Ball trucks broke, but didn't brake." The truckers took their cues from the combat forces, which, by the second week in September, had sent patrols into Germany on its frontier with Luxembourg and Belgium. There was a frenzy to deliver supplies to the front that was fueled by commanders desperate for materiel—the rules of the road be damned. MTB officers regularly reported seeing Jimmies racing along at speeds of up to 65 mph and the tractor trailers going at least 50 mph.

"The guys on the Red Ball. They were something," said Fred Reese, a mechanic with an ambulance unit assigned to the Red Ball. "They were going as fast as they could go. It was like they were on a suicide trip. When you'd see them coming you'd say, 'Here comes the Red Ball, let's move over.' They didn't stop for nothing. We always used to say, 'Hey, what's the big hurry?'"[2]

Red Ball drivers pushed on as fast as they could go, and many enjoyed the opportunity to "cowboy." Every soldier knew that most officers looked the other way as the trucks, many with perforated mufflers, roared down the highway. The drivers might be scolded by a colonel but never court-martialed for helping the cause. General Patton would be more likely to give them a medal than a reprimand.

"They really kept us going," James Rookard said. "We started driving in the morning and kept right on driving. Most of the time, you couldn't stop because there was always somebody right behind you."[3]

"You'd go up and dump off and come back," Herman Heard noted. "But you could understand. The infantry needed supplies."[4]

The rush to deliver materiel to the front seriously disrupted the convoy system. Regulations required that trucks travel in groups of sixteen or more, but less than a third of the vehicles did so during the first weeks of the Red Ball. Speed was so essential that trucks frequently loaded up and took off singly or in small groups to race to the front rather than wait for all of the Jimmies in a convoy to load. Often, it took several days to load an entire convoy.

The French picked up on the urgency of the Red Ball. Articles in French newspapers publicized the importance of the operation to French citizens who often strayed onto the one-way route in their personal vehicles. One newspaper caught the spirit of the frantic advance:

> At the front soldiers are waiting for guns and gasoline, bombs and bullets, and many other military essentials. The Red Ball convoys carry these supplies over the Red Ball Highway. That's why they've got to go through fast—not tomorrow—but right now. Thousands of lives may be sacrificed by a few seconds of needless delay.[5]

Speeding was part of the mystique of the Red Ball. "Push 'em up there," was a popular slogan in the ETO, and the Army pushed both men and trucks beyond their limits. For many Red Ball drivers, 40 mph was slow, and Rookard and others often drove at 60 or better. Drivers and mechanics frequently removed the governors, which regulated speed, from beneath the carburetors. The penalty for removing a governor could be severe, so a driver or mechanic often lifted the butterfly valve from the governor housing and left the housing in place beneath the carburetor to make it appear as if the valve were still in place.

Mechanic Paul Anderson perfected the practice of removing the governor:

> It would cut in at 52 miles an hour and come hell or high water that's all the truck would do until we operated on them—every one of them. Whenever I got the chance, I'd lift the carburetor off the motor, take two screws out, and pull out the governor.[6]

A Jimmy without its governor could roll along at speeds of 70 mph when empty and on a good road. Because most trucks were heavily laden, they could not go that fast but the drivers made every effort to do so.

Many drivers were going so fast that they didn't need an irate colonel to slow them down. Speed, combined with reckless driving, did it for them. One youthful driver dislocated the fingers on his hand when the steering wheel spun violently after the truck hit a pothole at high speed.

Several veterans remembered a steep hill on the Red Ball Highway where the road veered 90 degrees to the left at the bottom. Signs warned truckers to slow down and slide into low gear when they came down the decline. Many ignored the warning, and the curve was the site of numerous wrecks.[7] One veteran watched smoke pour from the brakes of Jimmies as the drivers attempted to slow the speeding vehicles on that hill.

Chester Jones, who served on the Red Ball as a staff sergeant with the 3418th QM Truck Company, spoke of an accident in a small French village that typified the kind of crashes that regularly occurred on the route as the result of speed and reckless driving:

> The road was one S curve after another. Boswell apparently decided to pass the truck ahead of him on a curve as we entered the town. He couldn't quite make the turn and hit one of those cement telephone poles, shearing it off. In some manner the wires held the upper part of the pole and swung it right into the cab where Boswell was sitting. . . . All of us ran back to Boswell's truck, which was about midway in the convoy; he didn't need first aid. Half his head had been caved in by the pole.[8]

One Army report noted dryly: "Wreckless driving was not the motto on the Red Ball."[9]

Speed did not kill or injure just Americans. German POWs sometimes were the victims. Robert Emerick said:

We often came back with German POWs. One time, they loaded so many in the back of a 2½-ton truck they all had to stand. This one crazy sucker in our outfit drove like a maniac. He got the truck going as fast as it would go. He came down off a grade and made a turn at the bottom and the whole side went out. Two Germans were killed and there were a lot of broken bones.[10]

Weight restrictions were ignored as well. The Jimmy originally was designed to carry a 2½-ton load, but prior to the Normandy invasion, the Transportation Corps permitted it to carry up to 5 tons to help compensate for the truck shortage. Those officers who followed regulations were ridiculed. Robert Emerick was required to carry an exact 5-ton load of 105- and 155-mm artillery shells to the front. "People would laugh when they saw us driving with so few shells."

Combat officers fumed at such light loads. SOP (standard operating procedure) be damned, the combat troops needed the supplies. Most trucks were dispatched overloaded, often dangerously so.[11]

Reese saw Red Ball trucks carrying ammunition boxes stacked above the top of the truck bed gates. The loads were so heavy that the trucks swayed back and forth as they sped down the highway. "They'd go down those damned highways, and when they got to a dip in the road the boxes would bounce around and flop out of the truck."[12]

Trucks held to the middle of the highway to maintain better control because the shoulders often dropped precipitously into gullies. If an overloaded truck ventured too close to the edge, it could easily topple into a roadside ditch.

Exhaustion was a companion closer than the assistant driver, who most likely was asleep. Trucks fell apart or ground to a halt for lack of proper care on the Red Ball. Men were a different matter. They didn't fall apart—they fell asleep. Sleep became an obsession for the drivers, and they struggled against it even as they succumbed to its grip.

The magazine *Yank* presented Red Ball drivers in a heroic light: "Truck drivers have worked 20 hours a day, and when their trucks zigzagged, they stopped, splashed water on their faces and drove on." The *Yank* writer added, "They carried their duffel bags with them and slept on piles of ruins which had scarcely cooled from the heat of battle."[13]

Hardly. Red Ball drivers could not stop. The men had to drive on.

"God, it was awful. Sometimes I felt like screaming. You couldn't sleep and they wouldn't let you stop," said Red Ball driver Booker Nance.[14] "The only time you could get decent sleep was when you got back to your company area." That might not be for days, even weeks. "You'd get so sleepy, you felt like you were drunk," Herman Heard noted.[15]

Driving in a somnolent haze, the men somehow steered their trucks down the narrow highways of Normandy into Ile de France, over the Seine into eastern France, through Champagne and Lorraine. They were shaken back to consciousness and reality by the jolt from a pothole left from a bomb or shell. Many Red Ball drivers were awakened as their trucks careened off the highway, headed for a ditch or utility pole, or bumped through a farmer's fields.

Red Ball drivers perfected the art of switching seats while their trucks were in motion on the road. The ritual, practiced often on the Red Ball, was one of the tricks of the trade that kept the convoys together. The assistant driver slid across the seat and under the driver as the two exchanged positions and continued driving. If the exchange was carried out with precision, a foot was always on the gas pedal.

Emerick said:

> I don't know of anybody who didn't fall asleep. Every so often you'd see a truck wander out of the convoy and somebody would holler, "He's asleep." The men in the convoys would blast their horns to awaken the driver of the drifting truck. I dozed off once. When you fall asleep in a 2½-tonner, you

release the pressure on the gas feed and the truck would start to drift back and out of the convoy. I woke up and was down in a ditch heading for one of those cement telephone poles. I hit a bump. That's what brought me to. That's when I heard horns blowing and knew my buddies in the convoy were trying to wake me up. It was hairy at times because you were driving so darn many hours.[16]

John Houston recalled the daily grind:

We ran through summer, fall, and winter, through snow, ice, and rain. Guys were falling asleep all the time. You couldn't get enough rest. I remember falling asleep on top of a jeep hood when it was raining like hell. I didn't know the difference.[17]

There were no formal rest areas where men could sleep. "Whenever possible, we stopped by the side of the road to take a pee or get five or ten minutes of sleep. Then we'd get back in and keep going," Rookard said.[18]

In desperation, many drivers pulled off the road for a catnap rather than attempt to make it back to their company areas. Red Ball trucks parked on the shoulders and sleeping drivers were concerns for MTB officers, who envisioned a more smartly run operation. Col. Clarence W. Richmond, MTB commander, ordered all Red Ball officers to eliminate the practice.

When a man was about to fall asleep at the wheel, however, the only alternative was to pull off the highway. Kenneth Duncan, who drove a wrecker for the 4267th QM Truck Company, stopped one night to sleep in a nearby field. The area still contained pockets of German stragglers, so Duncan took his rifle and curled up some distance from his truck in the underbrush. He was awakened the next morning by a man attempting to wrestle his boots from his feet. Duncan jumped up and grabbed his rifle as the terrified man backed away and screamed, "Nix shoot, nix shoot." He was a French farmer who thought he would liberate a pair of boots from a "dead" soldier.[19]

Charles Barber, a volunteer driver, drove for three days and four nights without sleep on the Red Ball. "We catnapped while they loaded us up. But as far as stretching out and falling asleep, forget it. You just fell asleep in the cab."[20]

When convoys were stalled in traffic, the drivers dozed, their heads slumped over the steering wheel. A jolt from the truck in front, as it backed up to tap the front bumper of the truck behind, was the signal that the convoy was on the move again.

One driver in Barber's company fell asleep and crashed into the 2½-ton truck in front. He smashed the lead vehicle's trailer but did not put his own truck out of commission. The drivers jumped out, threw the trailer into the roadside ditch, and drove on.

Nighttime travel was risky at speeds attained on the Red Ball, particularly when the only light was from the cat eyes. Emerick was mesmerized by "those damned little blackout lights. We would pick up the MSR [main supply route] outside Paris and drive through the night. You drove so long and all you were watching were those cat eyes. It drove you blind. It was like hypnosis and made it very easy to fall asleep."[21]

Everyone had his own way of staying awake. Some would sing. Others would talk with the assistant driver. If the men were lucky, they could stop at one of the few rest camps set up along the Red Ball Highway.

The trucks were often on the road for such long periods that drivers were always hungry. Most drivers carried their own rations and ate them on the road. Many trucks were loaded with ration boxes, and the drivers frequently snitched rations off the back as the MPs looked the other way. One Red Ball driver kicked ration boxes off the truck to feed demoralized MPs who were stuck at an intersection and hadn't been relieved or resupplied for days.

The drivers became proficient at eating while on the road by opening a ration tin and devouring the contents before chucking tin and top onto the highway. This habit of discarding ration tins on the route almost brought the Red Ball to a halt. The sharp-edged metal destroyed thousands of tires before the Army ordered the practice stopped.

Emerick ate the same bland ration diet of hash, stew, or beans —always cold. Everyone craved a hot meal, so drivers took to placing ration tins on the exhaust manifold to heat them up, but they could leave the tins there for only a few minutes. Emerick stuck a tin on the manifold and took off, forgetting to remove the container. A few miles down the road, he heard a muffled explosion up front, but he couldn't stop and break away from the convoy. When he returned the truck to the company motor pool for servicing, he received an earful from the first sergeant.

"What the hell have you been doing under this hood?!"[22]

DAILY LIFE
ON THE RED BALL

Life on the Red Ball was austere. "We still lived in tents," wrote one veteran of the 894th Ordnance HAM (Heavy Auto Maintenance) Company assigned to the Red Ball. "Beds were a civilian luxury, but some of the boys had constructed canvas cots and various adulterated throwbacks of vague design."[1]

Men pitched tents over their foxholes and slept in the holes to protect themselves against the possibility of air or ground attacks. Even in relatively secure areas, there were constant reminders of war and the 894th historian reported on its many inconveniences:

> The artillery kept booming so regularly and constantly that we wondered where the ammunition was coming from. There was a 90 MM A.A. [antiaircraft] gun in the next field. The whole earth sunk one foot the first time that went off and left us stranded in mid-air. "Better get into the foxhole before the flak comes down."[2]

During the summer, Red Ball units occasionally were housed in old barracks, schools, and other public buildings. Charles Stevenson's company bivouacked in a chateau along the Red Ball route that was owned by a marquis who was upset when his daughter became the object of one soldier's affections.[3] The men of K Company, 3630th QM Truck Company, were also housed in a chateau in the town of Gambais before dispersing to the homes of townspeople.[4]

By the first week in September, cold weather was forcing most units to find quarters indoors. It was a shock to many GIs, accustomed to longer, hotter summers in the States, particularly in the South, to find the leaves turning and the air becoming chilly by 1 September.

"The warm, dry summer is giving way to a wet chill fall. There is talk of stoves, heavy underwear and billets," Corporal Brice wrote on 6 September.[5]

The 3909th QM Truck Company moved into former French Army barracks on the outskirts of Dreux. I Company was billeted in a rambling farmhouse in a small village about five miles west of Nancy. Brice recorded the move:

> We are looking forward to this change from the "Great Outdoors." There were signs of considerable fighting in days past. Battle scars abound. Most windows have been shot out, iron bars have been twisted and torn from their bases in the concrete window sills, ceilings are pitted with bullet holes and the north wall has two very large shell holes torn in it.[6]

Wintry weather brought with it the old demon of mud that combined with ice and snow to make the roads slippery and dangerous. I Company's trucks were involved in five accidents in one night, more than it had experienced during the drive across France.

Through it all, the trucks rolled on. The 146th's historian noted the unit's daily routine:

> Round the clock non-stop convoys of trucks of all shapes and sizes thunder along a one-way network of highways across France, giving no respite to overloaded trucks and precious little rest for their drivers. Every day commanders from the First, Third, and Seventh armies would call their needs into headquarters and be evaluated. They in turn called the supply depots

at the beach as to who gets what and where to deliver. . . . We drove day and night [on the Red Ball] and went into blackout the last ten miles up to the enemy lines. Our outfit ran as two separate sections each with a wrecker and mechanics. The trucks ran 24 hours a day, seven days a week. We drove without assistant drivers and were allowed one hour to change drivers, throw off flats etcetera at our company area situated about halfway on the return leg. We had to make a round trip without sleep, and by the time the front was at the German border the beach was 600 miles behind and we drove 48 to 54 hours without sleep.[7]

After every move, the men of I Company who stayed behind in the company area had to set up shop once again. "The activity of the day is digging. Take your choice, ditches, foxholes, latrines and garbage pits," wrote Corporal Brice. He recorded five separate moves between mid-August and mid-September. On 15 September, I Company settled in on the World War I battlefield at Verdun. "We set up camp in a wooded area beyond the town of Étain. This area is itself a myriad of dugouts, trenches and old barbed wire from that holocaust [World War I]."[8]

The Army established major bivouac areas along the Red Ball Highway, one centered around the town of Alençon and another in the vicinity of Chartres. The huge transportation hub and rest area around Alençon was home base for some one hundred trucking companies and twenty-two thousand service troops after the breakout from Normandy. These areas provided beds, mess halls, and medical care for the men and heavy duty maintenance and new drivers for the vehicles.[9]

Many of the truck companies assigned to the Red Ball established their headquarters around Alençon with each company's headquarters divided into two sections, one to administer to trucks heading toward Paris and the other to handle vehicles heading back to the Normandy area.

The original plan was for drivers to pull into the Alençon area for rest periods ranging from an hour to several days to take advantage of the cots, hot meals, entertainment, and coffee dispensed by the Red Cross workers. In reality, however, the pace of the war was such that the drivers had little time for the recreation and entertainment facilities.

The memories of Alençon were fleeting. The drivers were so constantly on the move that 146th historian Bass noted that the men remembered only that the unit was set up in a field somewhere near the town. "The quickening pace of the advance was felt by the men of the 146th who were hardly allowed time to orientate themselves. . . . We wandered around, we were a bunch of damned gypsies, whenever they needed something hauled and they could use a truck company or a few trucks—they sent us there."[10]

But there were good times, too, as the 894th historian noted:

> In spite of it, we ate, slept at times, received free PX [post exchange] rations and saw a U.S.O. [United Service Organizations] show starring Little Caesar, the tough guy, Edward G. Robinson. We had a band from the beach and an occasional movie. . . . We ate but it was an extremely arduous task to remove the yellow jackets from the food, and sometimes you'd feel that you might as well eat them too.[11]

The Americans bivouacked around Alençon were both irked and amused by the curious French who flocked from miles around to see these big, friendly GIs with all their goods and equipment. One soldier reported that the French were "very nosy," and the Americans found themselves curiosities to the local people.

The historian for the 513th QM Group wrote that the Alençon hub was like theater to the French:

> Like Hollywood stars we had no private life. The more "off limits" signs we put up, the more they were disregarded as whole families pilgrimaged to the orchard where the first American troops to settle down were stationed. After solemnly shaking hands with all and asking the preliminary "Got any gum or

chocolate," they would spread out and enjoy themselves. They watched us eat, they watched us work, and they peered into our tents to see how we lived. We washed ourselves and our clothing to an appreciative audience. Some brave souls, curious to see what was going on behind that "screen" which was getting so much usage, ventured to peep under the canvas. With a shrug of their shoulders, they seemed to say they preferred their own casual way of answering nature's call.[12]

Discipline can be a problem in any soldiers' rest areas, and the Alençon bivouacs were no exception. The situation was sufficiently chaotic that Colonel Richmond convened a meeting of his battalion and group commanders on 2 September and demanded that they regain control of their men:

> In all these towns and villages in our bivouac area, there are literally hundreds of trucks out there at night. . . . And how they get out of the bivouac areas without the knowledge of the company commanders, I don't know. We have no mounted passes, we issue no individual recreational passes, and no trucks should be out of the bivouac area individually. IT MUST STOP. . . .
> All towns are "Off Limits." We have only one thing in mind at the present time, and that is to roll freight forward, and nothing else must enter our minds or the minds of the soldiers. We are doing everything we know how to do—just that and nothing more.[13]

Drunkenness and unauthorized absences were particular problems in many trucking units, including those in the 514th. Corporal Brice noted that three men from I Company were reduced to private after an illegal night on the town.[14]

The men of C Company, like others, had become masters at sneaking trucks out after dark or in persuading guards to look the other way. "We'd take a weapons carrier, roll it down the hill and once we got it past the officers or the guards we'd start it up and go anywhere we wanted," Chappelle said.[15]

Jack Blackwell sneaked into Paris without leave, as did many GIs who took illegal time from the Red Ball to visit the city. "About five or six of us decided to go AWOL [absent without leave] to Paris for the night since we weren't on duty till the next afternoon," wrote Red Ball veteran Philo Rockwell King III. They hitched a ride with a French trucker who sold them cognac for the trip into the city. The men groped around a dark city and pitch-black subways until they found a little bistro where there were women and dancing. He continued:

> What an extraordinary change this gayety was from the ruins we had seen all along the way—towns like Ste. Mère Église and St. Lô. One of my pals who found looking for girls was more interesting than trying to talk to people at the bar eventually found two ladies of the evening. They guided us to a nearby hotel, then it turned out we simply didn't have enough money for the services of the ladies, so my buddy and I slept in one room and the babes somewhere else.[16]

MPs were everywhere in Paris looking for AWOL soldiers. One GI from the Red Ball traveled to Paris on a weekend pass. He had settled in for the night in a bed with clean sheets when MPs barged into his room on a routine search for AWOL soldiers.

A sergeant from C Company was almost caught in an MP roundup at a bordello near Paris. To escape the dragnet, the sergeant jumped out on a ledge and waited, stark naked, for the police to leave. More than a half century later, he told his C Company buddies the end of the story: "Hell, I came back off the ledge in and finished my business."[17]

SIXTEEN

TEMPTATIONS AND BLACK MARKETS

There were temptations all along the Red Ball route. Men, women, and children were often standing on the sides of the road and begging from the rich and well-fed Americans as they rumbled by in monster trucks overladen with goods that the French had not seen in five years. The Yanks carried food, shoes and boots, clothing, and soft drinks—even candy. But the most sought after items were cigarettes and gasoline, and the French went to great lengths to acquire them.

Robert Emerick was startled to see a Frenchman scavenging for a few drops of spilled American gasoline for his cigarette lighter:

> We were waiting in line at a supply dump so we decided to clean our carburetor with gasoline from one of the extra jerri-cans we had on the truck. Some of the gas spilled and trickled into the gutter. This Frenchman comes out with an eyedropper and a little bottle. I wondered what the hell he was doing so I asked him. He said the gas was for his *briquette*—lighter. I said bring the damned bottle over here and I filled it up for him."[1]

"The French would try to sell you wine and we would give them cigarettes for it," James Rookard said.[2] Charles Stevenson said that he was "afraid to stop for a pee call along the road to Dinan because everybody came running out with bottles of wine and I was afraid my troops would all get bombed."[3]

Lt. William Harnist led his platoon of I Company Jimmies through cheering throngs in Rennes on the mission to deliver "repple depples" to the 4th Armored Division fighting its way across the Breton Peninsula. "Going through Rennes was like Lindbergh going down Fifth Avenue. We were the first American troops these people had seen and they were all out celebrating. It was really something, the wine and the gals all over the trucks." Harnist was so confused by all the hoopla that he failed to take a critical turn and did not realize his mistake until he was on the other side of town. He had to turn his troops around for another run through the gauntlet of delirious townspeople.[4]

The greatest temptation of all for the Red Ball troops was the French girls. "Sometimes girls would come up close to your truck and ask you certain things, you know, if you wanted to take care of business. I had what they wanted and they had what I wanted," one driver said.[5]

It was not uncommon for trucks to peel off the Red Ball "to take care of business" with French girls. "If you knew where you were going, some of the drivers would stop and do what they had to do and catch up with the convoy later on," the Red Ball veteran said.[6]

Many Americans were smitten by Frenchwomen whom the drivers would see daily standing by the highway, cheering on the trucks, and throwing smiles at the drivers. "We chalked slogans on our vehicles, which attracted enough demoiselles to entertain us at pauses," wrote Philo Rockwell King III.[7] All drivers heard the rumors about the good times a driver and assistant driver could have during a ten-minute break. Many of the men in C Company checked out the women, as did the members of other Red Ball units.

When five men in Stevenson's unit came down with gonorrhea, all company personnel returning from leave were required to take sulfa pills or a shot of penicillin. "Whenever they logged back in from a pass, we made them take five or six sulfa pills or a shot. They'd swear up and down they hadn't done anything. But they had orders to take the pills," Stevenson said.[8]

France, with its tradition of prostitution, was a new experience for many American troops, black and white. James Bailey was perplexed by the long line of American soldiers on a street in Cherbourg shortly after the port city was captured. When Bailey wondered aloud to his jeep companion why all the men were in line, he was told that they were awaiting their turn in a bordello. "I'd never seen anything like that before."[9]

A group from one truck company "bought" a house of prostitution in a town near Paris in which they were bivouacked. The men found themselves frequenting the house so often that they purchased a block of time for the entire company and each man acquired a certain number of visits for his money.

The distractions of women were known at regimental headquarters and even at higher commands. The 514th noted in reports that too many trucks were making unauthorized detours for sexual encounters.

If the temptations of the French women were great, those of the black market were even greater. Black market theft was a serious problem on the Red Ball. "There was enough material lost on the black market that it slowed down the war effort," said one C Company member, who requested anonymity. "Some of the theft was organized; much of it was guys just dabbling," he said.[10]

Emerick was surprised by one unlikely dabbler, a lieutenant in his own outfit. Moments after Emerick filled the Frenchman's lighter and bottle, as noted earlier, another civilian approached:

> He had seen me give gas to this other guy and he asked, "GI, you sell gas?" I said maybe, what'll you pay? He said 5,000 francs for a five-gallon can, which was one hundred dollars in those days. He started to move away because the lieutenant came up in a jeep. I told the lieutenant that the Frenchman wanted to buy a jerrican. The lieutenant asked if there were any extra cans on the truck. I said yeah, and he asked what are you getting for it. I said one hundred dollars. He said, "Sell it to 'em." He went on down the road and came back with a couple of cans and sold them to the Frenchman.[11]

A few Red Ball truckers weren't selling just a jerrican or two. They were selling entire truckloads of containers and the truck as well. "I sold everything I could get my hands on," said one Red Ball veteran, who asked for anonymity. "I'd sell it to the French. You could go into town and stop on the street and sell a whole truck if you wanted to."[12]

It was not difficult to dispose of a truck. With thousands of them on the Red Ball, no one could keep an accurate accounting of their locations at any given time. Also, many trucks, sometimes entire platoons of them, were on detached service and not under the control of their parent units.

One Red Ball veteran spoke of how easy it was to steal:

> They didn't keep any inventory of trucks. They didn't keep an inventory on anything else either. We'd go to the depot and get loaded up and there was nobody with a check list of the supplies being loaded. The Army had no idea how much of what was on each truck.[13]

Straggling contributed to black market theft. Without discipline, drivers dropped out of convoys anywhere along the Red Ball's 450-mile length and disappeared to sell their loads. The G-4 history reported that transport officers considered using motorcycle patrols to round up stragglers and placing more noncommissioned officers (NCOs) in the trucks to keep the convoys together.[14]

It was not uncommon for drivers in some units to report to MPs that their trucks and their loads had been "stolen," often under mysterious circumstances. Richard Bass recorded an incident involving theft in the 146th QM Truck Company:

> When we were on the Red Ball we did have a guy steal a truck out of the convoy, he went to Paris, I think he sold the gasoline by the five-gallon can. He had lots of money, he invested in a brothel, I don't think he bought it . . . but in a matter of a few days the MPs picked him up.[15]

Trucks broke down and were repaired elsewhere or were wrecked miles from their company areas. All a soldier had to do was straggle back to his company area and report that his truck had struck a mine or been strafed by enemy aircraft. The authorities could do little to verify the report. Red Ball drivers involved in the black market would sometimes follow a buddy and give him a ride back to base after a truck had been sold. At the height of the pursuit, it was an easy matter to claim that a load of jerricans had been hijacked by Patton's raiding parties.

The majority of the Red Ball drivers—honest soldiers doing their best to help win the war—had to be vigilant whenever and wherever they parked their trucks. Merle Gutherie was part of a twenty-truck convoy making a night stop at a restaurant in a French town on the Red Ball route to Paris:

> We were in the restaurant and here were some GIs unloading some boxes from our trucks. We ran out and caught them, and I said, "We're taking this stuff to the guys on the front and you rear-echelon SOBs are trying to take it away." They thought they were dead, and they almost were. I put a forty-five in one guy's middle and he thought I was going shoot him, and I damn near did.[16]

Trucks often were "requisitioned" by officers from units that needed instant transport. Vehicles were stopped and the driver informed by a higher-ranking officer that his vehicle was now under a different command. This practice was so common that Lieutenant Harnist carried orders from Third Army headquarters that his trucks were not to be requisitioned by anybody for any reason. Part of I Company's job was to move Patton's headquarters on an instant's notice. Harnist recounted:

> Some smart-ass captain walked up to me one day and says, "I'm taking four of your trucks. The hell you are, SIR. I pulled out my authorization slip that showed that unless he had written authority from a division commander or higher-ranking officer,

these were my trucks and NO ONE was going to take them. I told him that Georgie Patton was not turning them loose. The captain turned on his heel and walked away.[17]

There was no secret where many of the lost trucks on the Red Ball wound up. Brig. Gen. Pleas B. Rogers, commanding the Seine Section, COMZ, noted in a statement in *Stars and Stripes* that "when General Patton's tanks reached the Siegfried Line and ran dry, Army trucks were backed up the whole length of the Champs Elysées with GI's selling gas by the canful and cigarettes by the carton. . . . Those trucks were Red Ball trucks."[18]

In January 1945, *Newsweek* reported the effects of the black market: "Gasoline trucks are sometimes hijacked (by bands of outlaws) but if the drivers are cooperative they simply drive their trucks into underground garages, sell 1,000 gallons of gasoline for $5,000 or sell the truck as well and pocket another $1,000. In Paris alone, 2,000 military vehicles have been stolen."[19]

The theft of military vehicles reached such proportions that a driver had to remove the rotor arm from the distributor when he left the vehicle unattended; otherwise, the jeep or truck would be gone when he returned. These precautions created another black market specialty, rotor arms, which were selling for $40 apiece—about $800 to $1,000 in today's dollars. Thieves with the proper rotor arms could steal any military vehicle on the road.[20]

By the beginning of 1945, the Army estimated as many as nineteen thousand AWOL GIs in France, the majority of whom were in Paris, and MPs were arresting up to three hundred a day. To survive on the lam, AWOL GIs often turned to theft and joined gangs that thrived on stealing military materiel flowing into Paris or headed to the front. The Army assigned four thousand MPs to the Paris region in an effort to clamp down on black marketeers. This was in stark contrast to the seven hundred MPs required to maintain order in London before the invasion. Some of the MPs assigned to Paris could have been used directing traffic on the Red Ball Highway.

The magazine *Yank* wrote an extensive exposé about the black market:

> The biggest profits were in gasoline and trucking rather than rations, so the GI gangsters switched to these rackets. The French underworld was quick to make friends with them. In bars, cafes, hotels, and houses of prostitution in the Montmartre and Montparnasse areas, the French gangsters made deals with the AWOLs. The GIs agreed to sell gasoline and other commodities wholesale to the fences and they in turn would find retail outlets. The first AWOLs were gradually joined by others. Some of the new recruits came from the Red Ball Highway, the trucking route then in operation from Cherbourg forward. They brought with them truckloads of gas that found a ready market."[21]

One driver of the 146th QM Truck Company narrowly escaped court-martial because a crate in a load of cigarettes had been emptied of its contents. Richard Bass recounted the experience of Fred Cox of the 146th:

> Stevedores loaded my truck so I watched them putting these cases on. They're made out of wood and you got so you knew the color code. Right on the corner they'd have one color or two colors or a combination, and it seemed like green and black was PX supplies like cigarettes. These boxes held fifty cartons of cigarettes and ten packs in a carton. On the black market a case was worth a thousand dollars. We drove on, Sergeant Hollett rode with me and I drove the first truck in the convoy up to Liège, Belgium, pulled into the ware house and Negro troops there unloaded us—a Negro lieutenant in charge of them. They got down to the bottom layer of my truck and the box right in the middle, they picked it up out of there and the Lieutenant said to me, "What's the meaning of this, soldier?" and the darned box had a hole in it and it was empty. Somebody made a small hole big enough to get a carton out. When the guys put

'em on of course the hole was down. I didn't see it. I saw 'em put
a box on, I didn't know it was empty. So this Negro Lieutenant
he's gonna get me for stealing them cigarettes.[22]

Cox and Sergeant Hollett persuaded the officer that there
was no way Cox could have stolen the cigarettes. They had
been loaded by another company. If Cox had stopped to steal
the cartons, not only would he have had to unload the entire
truck but, as the lead truck, he would have had to stop the
entire convoy.

In September, the troops in the ETO experienced a serious
cigarette shortage. The weekly ration for each soldier was seven
packs, but the black market had siphoned off so many American-
brand cigarettes that each soldier's quota was met only by adding three packs of captured "German, Turkish-type weeds."

Morale in the combat units was affected, and the fallout
reached as far back as SHAEF (Supreme Commander of the
Allied Expeditionary Forces) headquarters and Supreme Commander Eisenhower himself, who ordered an immediate investi-
gation into the matter. Some 77 million packs of cigarettes a
month were slated for distribution in the European Theater, yet,
in one thirty-day period, only 11 million packs had reached their
destination. A *Yank* reporter noted that "in the French bars,
cafes, and other public places, plenty of civilians were smoking
popular-brand American cigarettes."[23]

There was no real mystery to the cigarette shortage. Small for-
tunes were being made by selling them on the black market. A
pack of cigarettes that sold in the PX for five cents brought as
much as $2.40 on the black market. Any Red Ball driver knew
the value of his cargo if it was gasoline or cigarettes.

For many of the men, the motivation to steal goods from the
Red Ball was the desire to send money home to families or sweet-
hearts. "Before I married my wife I used to send her quite a bit of
money," one Red Ball veteran said. So many troops were sending
money home that some military post offices restricted the amount

of cash that the GIs could ship home. "They figured it came from the black market," the Red Ball veteran said. Much of it did.[24]

Whatever the reason for the pilferage on the Red Ball, those veterans who did not partake point out that some theft occurred during the war wherever troops had access to huge quantities of materiel. It just did not make the newsreels.

SEVENTEEN

SECRET WEAPON

The truck was the secret weapon in the ground war in the European Theater, but it was one distinctly lacking in romance and glory. Even the name had no ring, although the troops squeezed some panache out of the deuce-and-a-half by affectionately nicknaming it the "Jimmy." Without the truck, nothing would have moved—neither tanks nor infantry. Even the artillery would have been silenced by a lack of shells. The armies would have advanced at the pace of horse-and-wagon trains, and World War II could have become a conflict of attrition similar to World War I.

Railroads had been the prime suppliers of the armies during World War I, but they are not conducive to mobile operations because they are tied to fixed routes. The truck made the mechanized and mobile warfare of World War II possible.

The Germans were, and often still are, hailed as the masters of mechanized warfare, which employs tanks and motorized infantry. Of the more than three hundred divisions in the Wehrmacht, however, few were mechanized. The bulk of the German Army of World War II was largely supplied by wagon trains, even to the end, and its infantry marched or rode trains or even used bicycles. During the war, the Germans drafted some 2,800,000 horses into military service, whereas the American Army maintained only 56,403 mules and horses and virtually ceased acquiring them after 1943. Many of the horses in the U.S. Army were in the remaining cavalry divisions that still used them at the outset of the war, but these divisions were stripped of their horses by 1943. Few, if any, American units were supplied by horse or mule except in mountainous terrain, such as in Italy.[1]

The famed blitzkrieg, the highly mobile, mechanized warfare with which the Wehrmacht defeated Poland in 1939, the Low Countries and France in 1940, and the Red Army in 1941 and 1942, was largely the work of the few German mechanized divisions. The statistics on the limited mechanization of the German Army are revealing, as well as surprising. Martin Van Creveld wrote:

> Of the 103 divisions available on the eve of war, 1939, just sixteen armored, motorized and "light" formations were fully motorized. The rest all marched on foot, and, though a complement of 942 motor vehicles (excluding motorcycles) was the authorized establishment of each infantry division, the bulk of their supplies was carried on 1,200 horse-drawn wagons. Even worse, all the 942 motor vehicles were organic to their units [they performed many functions independent of supply] and earmarked mainly for work inside the zone of operations.
>
> To bridge the distance from the depots to the railheads, only three transport regiments were available for the whole [German] Army, having between them some 9,000 men, 6,600 vehicles (of which twenty percent were expected to be undergoing repair at any moment) and a capacity of 19,000 tons. . . . One may note, however, that the allies in 1944 used no less than 69,400 tons of motor transport to support forty-seven divisions in France, but nevertheless suffered from a grave shortage [of trucking].[2]

The German Army also suffered severely from a lack of standardization in its motorized units. Van Creveld continued:

> The Germans in Russia used no less than 2,000 different types of vehicles, the spare parts required by those in the area of Army

Group Center alone numbering well over one million. In the winter of 1939–40, and again in that of 1940–41, it was necessary partly to demotorize units and services. This was in spite of the fact that, by the latter date, no less than eighty-eight German divisions—some forty percent of the total—were equipped with captured French material.[3]

Even as late as the Battle of the Bulge, the Germans were using captured or appropriated French equipment. In a film clip showing SS Lt. Col. Joaquin Peiper's advance through the Bulge, a French Citroën of 1930s vintage is seen trailing a German armored vehicle. Peiper commanded a battle group spearheading the drive on the northern flank of the Bulge.

The American Army in World War II truly became the world's most highly mobile and mechanized force largely because it was supplied by trucks. In fact, the Americans fielded the only Army capable of full mechanization. No other nation had the industrial capacity to produce so many trucks and other vehicles. Van Creveld asserted that "Germany's automobile industry was insufficiently developed to meet the needs of its Army."[4]

By war's end, the ratio of trucks to men in the American Army in the ETO was one vehicle for every four U.S. soldiers. Historians Henry C. Thompson and Lida Mayo reported that "in the later stages of World War II it was theoretically possible, if not feasible for practical reasons, to put an entire army on wheels—pile everyone into trucks, buses, ambulances, and other vehicles, and all take to the road at once."[5]

The Americans produced nearly 2½ million trucks or truck-type vehicles during World War II. If the nearly 600,000 trailers and semitrailers produced are added to this figure, around 3 million truck-type vehicles were manufactured for the war effort.[6]

The United States manufactured so many trucks that scores of thousands were shipped to other Allied armies, particularly the Red Army, under Lend-Lease during the war. The Soviets received mostly 2½-ton Studebakers that played a critical role in the defeat of the Germans in Russia.

Also, American trucks were of good quality and were both simple and rugged. The English military historian John Keegan, who was a schoolboy during World War II, was greatly impressed by the size and quality of the American trucks that he saw as a young lad:

> More striking still were the number, size and elegance of the vehicles in which they [the Americans] paraded about the countryside in stately convoys. The British Army's transport was a sad collection of underpowered makeshifts, whose dun paint flaked from their tinpot bodywork. The Americans traveled in magnificent, gleaming olive-green, pressed-steel, four-wheel–drive juggernauts, decked with what car salesmen would call optional extras of a sort never seen on their domestic equivalent—deep treaded spare tyres, winches, towing cables, fire extinguishers. They were towering six-by-sixes, compact and powerful Dodge four-by-fours and . . . tiny and entrancing jeeps.[7]

The standard American truck was the 2½-ton, six-by-six CCKW—or Jimmy—that had been developed by the Army in the late 1930s. It was the epitome of simplicity with little more than an engine and a transmission.

There were two basic cargo versions of the Jimmy. The one produced in greater numbers was designed with a 164-inch wheelbase without a winch and weighed 15,450 pounds. The smaller version came with a 145-inch wheelbase and weighed 15,350 pounds without a winch.

A breakdown of the number of American trucks produced during the war is as follows:

Light trucks (1 ton and under)	988,167
Medium trucks (1½ tons)	428,196
Light-heavy trucks (2½ tons)	812,262
Heavy-heavy trucks (over 2½ tons)	153,686
Semitrailers	59,731
Trailers	499,827
Tractors	34,272[8]

The military truck of World War II had come a long way in the twenty-six years since trucks were first used in combat by the American Army during the Mexican Expedition against Pancho Villa. In 1916, Gen. John J. Pershing's forces found the truck more versatile than the horse. It was simple to repair, could deliver nearly continuous service, did not need rest, and could rapidly supply the Army.

Lt. Omar N. Bradley, future commander of the American 12th Army Group, also learned the value of the truck firsthand while serving with Pershing. Bradley's 14th Regiment was transferred by rail from Washington state to the Mexican border area. The trip required five days of travel. Nearly a day of this time—twenty hours—was devoted to stopping the train and exercising the regiment's horses. Army regulations required that horses be exercised four out of every twenty-four hours.[9]

In 1919, the Army dispatched a cross-continental convoy to test the efficiency of the truck for supplying a fast-moving army. One of the junior officers on the expedition was Lt. Dwight D. Eisenhower. The tactical and strategic importance of the truck was not lost on the future Supreme Commander.[10]

By the early 1940s, the American Army had retired the horse and America's generals of World War II came to display a genius for movement using motor vehicles that was awe inspiring to friend and foe alike. Mobility was not limited to Gen. George S. Patton and his Third Army. The First Army's tanks and infantry under Gen. Courtney Hodges moved with equal rapidity. Patton's and Hodges's boss, General Bradley, had long been a student of Civil War Gen. William T. Sherman, a master of the war of movement. Bradley believed that "rapid, sweeping massed movement of forces deep into the enemy's heartland was the best way to destroy an enemy army."[11] The tank might lead the way, but it was supplied by trucks.

The American flare for trucking in World War II traced its origins to the vastness of the American continent. The Red Ball also grew out of the American experience of developing this giant nation. Highways were stitching the country together and were more economical in remote areas than the railroad. There were more four-wheeled motor vehicles in the United States in proportion to its population than anywhere else in the world. Prior to the war, the ratios were 1 to 70 people in Germany and 1 to 10 people in the United States.[12]

By the 1940s, the Americans understood the strategic value of the motor vehicle better than any other army, particularly those in Europe, which were more dependent on railroads. In a September 1944, article on the Red Ball titled "The Miracle of Supply," *Time* magazine wrote that the Germans never anticipated the American Army's ability to supply its forces with such vast quantities of materiel. "The miracle could be stated in simple arithmetical terms: in the first one hundred days after D-Day, over 1,000,000 longtons of supplies (700,000 items) and 100,000 vehicles poured into France."[13]

Time dubbed the American genius for rapid supply "The North American Way." The article continued, "This miracle was in the American tradition, a tradition the Germans have never really understood. It was begotten of a people accustomed to great spaces, to transcontinental railways, to nationwide trucking chains, to endless roads and millions of automobiles."[14]

By the end of World War II, the United States had married the truck to its vast war-making potential and its extensive manpower resources to create the world's most highly efficient and destructive mechanized army. Gen. James Van Fleet described this new army that emerged in 1945:

> We Americans know how to command and move large forces, how to sustain in a major engagement. The only other army that knew how to do that was the German Army and we destroyed that Army. The British cannot do that. They have to plan and then shoot their works for several days and then stop and as Montgomery often said "tidy up the battlefield." This means rest, recuperation, resupply. That is very much the case of the Soviet Army. The Communist forces make a plan and give it supply that will maintain that offensive for perhaps a

week, but they have no capabilities of maintaining that offensive continuously, changing direction, stopping, moving backwards or, in the middle of the night, changing formation. The American Army is taught that the impetus of supply comes from the rear and the rear element of that support supplies the front lines with what it takes to keep moving in ammunition, men and weapons, food and medical services. Only the American Army can do that.[15]

And the Army did it, to a large degree, with the Jimmy.

James Rookard

James Chappelle (left) and James Rookard somewhere on the Red Ball in France in the fall of 1944.

James Rookard

Members of C Company of the 514th Truck Regiment. From left: James H. Bailey, Clarence Bainsford, Jack R. Blackwell, and John R. Houston (father of singer/actress Whitney Houston).

Members of Battery A, 4520th Anti-Aircraft Battalion, check their 40mm Bofors gun and other equipment during a break on a French highway in 1944. Antiaircraft units such as this one tried to protect Red Ball convoys from strafing attacks by Luftwaffe fighters.

Cpl. Charles H. Johnson of the 783d Military Police Battalion waves on a convoy bound for Alençon on the Red Ball Highway on 5 September 1944. To guide the drivers, the Red Ball route was lined with these signs, although most were not as elaborate.

Two-and-a-half-ton Jimmies set out onto the Red Ball Highway from a depot area in France loaded with 5-gallon jerricans filled with gas. In the first weeks of the breakout from Normandy, most of the gasoline that kept the armies going was delivered to the front this way. The trucks pass a jeep that will probably bring up the rear of the convoy. A jeep was also often positioned at the head of each convoy.

Mechanics labor over broken-down Jimmies. The efficiency of the Red Ball was threatened by the breakdown of thousands of trucks that were driven mercilessly.

Cab-over-engine, four-by-four tractors hauling trailers filled with gasoline pass along the Red Ball route somewhere in France, while an MP maintains the flow of traffic. The army used more trailers as the war progressed and they became available.

M.Sgt. Bennie Burns, Sgt. Vincent MacNeil, Sgt. Frank Mack, Pfc. Riggler McCutcheon, T.Sgt. John A. Barbee, and Sgt. Thomas G. Alexander clear mines in France. The threat of mines along the shoulders of Red Ball roads prompted trucks to travel in the middle of the road, particularly in areas recently liberated of Germans.

Hurry up and wait. Their vehicles loaded and ready to go, crewmen of a trucking unit await orders to move out. These truckers are white and possibly from one of the provisional trucking companies composed of volunteers from units not in the thick of the fighting. Black and white truckers seldom operated together, and fraternization between them was discouraged.

The inexorable flow of Red Ball Express trucks could only be made possible by constant maintenance. Nevertheless, breakdowns often hindered the convoys' progress.

T.Sgt. Sherman Hughes, T.Sgt. Hudson Murphy, and Pfc. Zacariah Gibbs, all of the 666th Quartermaster Truck Company, stand tall in front of their 2½ ton Jimmies after each had chalked up 20,000 accident-free miles carrying supplies to the front.

EIGHTEEN

THE JIMMY

To the Americans, the Jimmy was the best truck of World War II, as well as the mainstay of the Red Ball Express. Accolades came, and still come, from all quarters. The Jimmy was said to be durable; it was said to outperform its enemy counterparts and get the job done. Certainly without the Jimmy, it would have taken many more months to subdue Nazi Germany.

According to Thompson and Mayo, "The two-and-a-half–ton truck, a military adaptation of a commercial model, was an immediate success and remained unsurpassed as a general purpose vehicle throughout the war. 'I have seen nothing belonging to our enemies or our Allies that can compare with it,' wrote one combat observer."[1]

Was the Jimmy the best truck of the war? It undoubtedly was. The Germans were known to have had superb military equipment, well-designed and beautifully engineered tanks and trucks. But well-engineered vehicles are not necessarily better in war. Many mechanics believe that the Germans had a tendency to overengineer their military vehicles, including trucks. "They were made like Swiss watches, beautifully crafted,"said Robert ("Bob") Rubino, manager of the Motor Pool, an organization directed by Frank Buck of Bartonsville, Pa., that restores World War II military vehicles. As a mechanic, Rubino knows the truck intimately, and he restored his own 1941 version. Rubino added, "But when a Swiss watch runs over a mine it becomes junk, just like a Jimmy, no matter how well built."[2]

To give an example of superb but inefficient German military engineering, Rubino compared the difference between the tank-like tracks of an American half-track with those of its German counterpart. The American tracks essentially were two steel cables and reinforcing crossbars, all molded into a single unit by vulcanized rubber. They were simple, had a wear-life of about 1,500 miles, and were easily and cheaply removed and replaced.

The tracks on a German half-track, on the other hand, consisted of individual steel crossbars held together in a continuous track by a series of pins, with each pin held in place by a pair of needle bearings. There is no question in Rubino's mind that the German tracks were often better engineered, stronger, and longer lasting. In a combat situation, however, equipment is damaged and destroyed so quickly that "better" most often is that which is simple, inexpensive, and easily replaced.

The deuce-and-a-half, as the Jimmy was often called, was no mechanical marvel. If anything, it was the exact opposite. "The Jimmy was often regarded as a piece of junk. But that's why it was so good," Rubino remarked. It did its job and served its purpose in all theaters of war, and when it was no longer able to be driven, it was discarded, like junk. It then went to the salvage yard, where it became parts for another truck that was still serviceable.

The Army might have complained that there was less standardization in U.S. military trucks during World War II than was to be desired, but, compared with those of the German Army, the American Army's vehicles were highly standardized. If a deuce-and-a-half's engine or transmission failed, any other Jimmy in military service could provide the replacement parts. In fact, the Americans kept scores of thousands of Jimmies rolling in the ETO with cannibalized parts. When GIs were transported to war in a Jimmy, chances are that it was a composite of several trucks.

Some Jimmy parts, however, were not interchangeable. The trucks were being produced in such great numbers that the Army permitted the manufacture of two different drive lines. One was dubbed the banjo, and the other was the Timken or split drive line. They could not be swapped.

Various parts that fit the Jimmy also were compatible with other types of vehicles. The cab, windshield, seats, and instrument panel on the Ward-LaFrance wrecker, used extensively in the ETO, were interchangeable.

Its very simplicity, coupled with the advantage of interchangeability of many parts, made the Jimmy the best truck of the war. Gunther Ctortnik, a Viennese who owns numerous American and German trucks of World War II vintage, noted that the Germans constantly improved the quality and performance of their trucks during the war. In consequence, most parts were no longer interchangeable. "There were too many different types of parts for the German trucks," Ctortnik said. "This made maintenance very difficult. They were trying always to make the trucks better."[3]

The Jimmy might be likened to the Sherman tank. The Sherman's superiority lay in the fact that it was simple, easily manufactured, and mass produced. Technically and, in many respects, mechanically, it was inferior to the German Panther and Tiger, the best of the German tanks. Although the U.S. Army knew that it took a ratio of four Shermans to destroy one Panther or Tiger in battle, the Americans manufactured the Shermans by the tens of thousands while the Germans built the Panthers and Tigers by the few thousands. In the end, it was the simple, mass-produced Sherman that was still coming at the enemy—by the thousands.

In the same way, the deuce-and-a-half was the better truck. It had its faults, but these were often overcome and overlooked by the sheer numbers of 2½-ton trucks, more than 800,000, that were produced by American industry during World War II. The Jimmy just kept coming, relentlessly and endlessly, and no other country had the industrial capacity to produce so many trucks.

It was this ability to outproduce its enemies that most characterized the American way of war. Van Creveld noted, "It would

appear that the U.S. Army, backed by a gigantic productive engine . . . chose to regard war not so much as a struggle between
opposing troops but rather as one whose outcome would be decided largely by machines."[4]

The Jimmy was almost literally slapped together, and, as the
war progressed, the steel content of the truck was drastically
reduced. In an effort to conserve metal, the enclosed cab of hard
steel in the 1941 versions gave way to an open cab, bolted together, with canvas top and sides. The cargo bed went from solid
steel to heavy pieces of lumber.

The life expectancy of the truck was six to nine months, and
the engine, under optimal conditions, lasted only around 20,000
miles. In part, this was a function of the engine technology of
that day. The metals were softer, and motor vehicles were not
designed to travel the distances they do today. But few Jimmy
engines in the ETO would make 20,000 miles. "They were built
with the idea that they would either be blown up or wrecked,"
said Lee Holland, a truck historian who knows the vehicle well.
"The question was not how long can we make these trucks last,
but how many can we produce?"[5] During the Sicilian Campaign,
for example, the Army found that 54 percent of all its equipment, including trucks, was destroyed directly or indirectly
through enemy action.

The simplicity of the Jimmy helped extend its lifespan. Good
mechanics could remove the engine and attached transmission
in several hours. A new or rebuilt power train could be rein-
stalled in about the same amount of time. Mechanics with the
894th Ordnance HAM Company became so proficient that
they could completely rebuild an entire truck in seventy-two
hours.[6]

There was not much more in the engine compartment than
the motor and transmission. Added features under the hood
included the radiator, coil, starter motor, oil filter, oil pump,
breather for the crank case, and voltage regulator. That was it.
The Jimmy had none of the accoutrements of modern vehicles,
such as power steering, power brakes, and air conditioning.

The truck carried two cat eye blackout lights in the front along with a blackout driving light, the size of a small headlight, covered by a tin plate with a small slit for light to escape. In the rear, the truck carried two blackout taillights and one blackout stoplight. The rear blackout lights, about the circumference of a soup can, were red.

The Army also made the Jimmy simple to maintain. Various components in the engine compartment were painted red to alert drivers and mechanics to those parts needing constant attention. These included the oil and water caps and the oil dipstick. Lubrication joints around the truck were also painted red, and each truck carried a lube gun. On the front lip of every Jimmy hood, mechanics stenciled in yellow paint the word *Prestone* and the year in which the antifreeze had been added. The truck was able to operate on gasoline with an octane rating as low as sixty, but the Army's gas usually was around eighty octane.

Later in the war, the U.S. Army introduced the cab-over-engine (COE) version. In outward appearance, the COE model looked nothing like the standard Jimmy, but the power train and most of the truck's parts were identical. The drive line in the COE trucks was the banjo. The biggest difference between the two models was that the more vertical cab extended the cargo bed, from 9–12 feet in the two standard Jimmies to 15–17 feet in the two standard COE vehicles. The cargo bed's side panels on later models of the COE truck also flipped down so that the supplies could be palletized, loaded, and removed by forklift.

The clutch and transmission were considered by mechanics to be the Jimmy's weakest link. This was due in large part to the fact that the truck was originally a civilian truck adapted to military use. The transmission was not designed to haul thousands of pounds of materiel over shattered roads, day and night, week after week, and month after month in combat conditions. It was never made for life on the Red Ball Express.

"We had a lot of soldiers who were farmboys who didn't know how to drive a clutch truck," Holland said. "They didn't know when to downshift and this would cause the main shaft to snap when they were carrying too heavy a load in too high a gear."[7]

Rubino noted that the banjo drive line also was vulnerable to wear. "The banjo was an extremely cheap setup, all ball bearings with no tolerance adjustments. It was just slapped together and away you went, and after long periods of high speeds, 45 to 50 mph, the transfer case would shatter. But, in the war, everything was disposable."[8]

Although the Army had hundreds of thousands of trucks, it had even more transmissions and rear drive lines, and the way to keep a Jimmy rolling was to drop out the old part and put in a new or used one. Throughout the European theater, the Army maintained vehicle service yards, sometimes known as "Little Detroits," where trucks were rebuilt and refurbished. These stations also took new truck parts directly from U.S. factories and assembled them into new vehicles that were ready to move on the Red Ball Highway.

That the U.S. Army ever produced the Jimmy was something of a miracle. Historians Thompson and Mayo noted that "the history of the Army motor transport from World War I to World War II is largely the record of the quartermaster corps' unsuccessful efforts to achieve standardization."[9] During the period between the two wars, quartermaster officers were at the mercy of their civilian masters who stipulated that all contracts for military vehicles be awarded to the lowest bidder and who forbade the Army to "issue detailed engineering specifications for trucks. There was to be no Army truck of special design but only commercial trucks with a few military trimmings."[10]

Whenever the Army announced plans for a new vehicle, scores of auto and truck manufacturers sent in bids, and there were many more small auto manufacturers in those days. As the Army was required to accept the low bids, it was not long before the military had an amalgamation of trucks, some dating back to World War I. The number of vehicles mushroomed, as did the number of spare parts required to keep the fleet operating.

During the late 1920s and early 1930s, the Quartermaster Corps began assembling prototype trucks from civilian vehicle parts with the hope that they would form the basis for a few standardized trucks. Even these attempts had to be abandoned because of opposition, in part, from the Chief of Ordnance, who considered the plan impractical. Thompson and Mayo noted that "the prevailing view was that the Army should stay out of the business of manufacturing and assembling trucks, and should not carry out any automotive research and development. Appropriation acts in the middle thirties specifically forbade spending money for research on motor vehicle standardization."[11] By the mid-1930s, the Army maintained a fleet of 360 models of vehicles, which required an inventory of more than a million items of spare parts.

As late as 1939, the Army was still limited to purchases of trucks designed and made by civilians because it was believed that, in time of war, this was the fastest way to produce large numbers of vehicles for the military. But there was one important change. The War Department limited the number of Army trucks to five chassis types—½-ton, 1½-ton, 2½-ton, 4-ton, and 7½-ton. The Quartermaster Corps also urged manufacturers to standardize as many common automotive parts as possible, such as batteries, spark plugs, generators, fan belts, speedometers, and fuel tanks.

Six-wheel-drive trucks like the Jimmy existed in the civilian market prior to World War II but only in very small numbers. They were used in specialty areas, such as off-road work and oil drilling. Most were huge trucks, in the range of 6 to 20 tons, and seldom seen on the open road. The approach of World War II created interest in the development of a medium-weight 2½-ton truck with exceptional mobility for military use. Early versions of the truck were in the 2- to 3-ton range. In 1940, General Motors Corporation developed a 2½-ton truck that would become the GMC Jimmy of World War II and the Cold War era.

In 1940, the Army tested and approved three commercial truck types, the Dodge four-by-four, 1½ tons; the GMC six-by-six, 2½ tons; and the Mack six-by-six, 6 tons. According to Thompson and Mayo, "It earnestly requested authority to purchase these vehicles from the firms indicated instead of advertising for bids and awarding contracts to the lowest bidder. The purpose, it explained, was 'to take advantage of the lessons of motor vehicle maintenance learned from our World War experience,' and avert a breakdown of field maintenance in an emergency."[12] Once again, the request was denied. It wasn't until 1941, before Pearl Harbor, that the Army was permitted to negotiate contracts for the development and procurement of the vehicles that it wanted in its fleets of trucks.

The Jimmy that went to war in 1941 looked like a civilian vehicle with its hard cab and carlike windshield. In late 1941, contracts were issued for several thousand of these vehicles. Before the year was out, it was clear that the truck would be the workhorse of the Army and thousands more would be needed. By 1943, the vehicle had changed its appearance and was being styled like a military vehicle.

To a large extent, the Jimmy became the premier truck of the American Army in World War II because prewar transportation planners failed to recognize the need for a heavier truck, particularly for warfare in the ETO and North Africa. This shortsightedness has led some military historians to argue that had the American Army ordered more heavy trucks, it might have been able to supply its fast-moving armies in France and broken through the Siegfried line to defeat Germany months earlier. The heavies had a hauling capacity twice that of the Jimmy—from 5 to around 10 tons.

Army transport officers anticipated the need for large numbers of the big long-haul trucks but were unable to convince their superiors of the need in 1940–41. A few orders for the large trucks were placed with the Mack Manufacturing Co., the Federal Motor Truck Co., the Corbitt Company, the White Motor Co., and the Diamond T Motor Co., but the quantities were in the hundreds rather than the thousands.[13]

The heavies were COE "tractors" that could haul trailers loaded with 10 tons or more of supplies. There were several versions of the heavies. International manufactured a version in which only the rear duals were powered. Autocar and Federal built four-by-four versions in which both rear duals and front wheels were powered. The heavies were driven by an in-line 6-cylinder, 400–cubic-inch engine that was more powerful than the Jimmy's 270–cubic-inch motor. Most of the heavy trucks came with a soft top.

The heavies considerably reduced the loading times at rear and forward depots. When the Jimmies arrived at their destinations, truck and cargo had to wait to be unloaded and reloaded. The heavy trucks, on the other hand, could drop their trailers, hitch up to a preloaded trailer, and hurry back to the main depot, thus saving the Army countless hours in the delivery of supplies.

One of the most innovative truck designs of the war, and an offshoot of the Jimmy, was the DUKW. The truck's name came from the manufacturer's code for the vehicle D for 1942, U for utility, K for front-wheel drive, and W for two rear-driving axles.

The DUKW was developed as a vehicle to carry supplies and troops from ship to shore, with the ability to drive right onto the beach. The DUKW consisted of a watertight body on the chassis of a 2½-ton truck. It was 36 feet long and 8 feet wide and could accommodate fifty men or an equivalent load of supplies. On land, it could use all six driving wheels, like the Jimmy, and conventional steering gear. In the water, it made use of a propeller and a rudder. It could use both wheel and propeller drive when emerging from water onto land.

The DUKW was first used in the South Pacific to transfer cargo to shore and made its debut in the European Theater during the invasion of Sicily. Its service at Normandy was invaluable. These stubby water workhorses chugged for months between ships at anchor off the invasion beaches and the depots in the hedgerows of Normandy. In all some 21,147 DUKWs were manufactured during the war.

The 2½-ton truck remained in the U.S. military inventory for more than a half century after it was first introduced at the beginning of World War II. The World War II Jimmy was modified after the war into more powerful versions.

The original Jimmy stayed behind in many countries to become a part of numerous foreign armies. The Communist Chinese used Jimmies to defeat the Nationalists in their takeover of mainland China. The French used the Jimmy for years in their army, and it saw service in Indochina and in many parts of Africa.

To those who still own and drive the Jimmy, there is no other truck anywhere of the same vintage that is comparable. By some estimates, as many as ten to twenty thousand Jimmies remain in private hands around the world. As many as five thousand have been restored by collectors and museums. Not until the early 1990s were the last World War II Jimmies "surplused out" of European armies. The Norwegian military auctioned off the last of its stocks in 1993. In European armies, the trucks had been well maintained and most had been rebuilt at some point during the last half century.

Manuel Rogers, a collector of WWII vehicles who lives in Massachusetts, said that one eager buyer at the Norwegian auction apparently was a representative of the Iraqi military. Rogers said that a friend, who is a military vehicle collector, spotted several Jimmies with Norwegian auction numbers plainly visible in a CNN news tape depicting equipment in the Iraqi Army.

The thrill of buying a mint-condition Jimmy was nothing for Rogers compared with driving away in one. "When I bought that vehicle at auction, I was driving it out of active duty for the first time in fifty years. Believe me, it raised bumps on the back of my neck."[14]

NINETEEN

THE UBIQUITOUS JERRICAN

The humble jerrican doesn't rate much attention in the annals of World War II, even though this 5-gallon container contributed quite a bit to victory and became an enduring symbol of the war.

The jerrican also could be called the symbol of the Red Ball Express. Trucks carried jerricans by the millions in their cargo bays, and the ubiquitous can was strapped on the backs of jeeps, on the running boards of Jimmies, and even to the fronts of tanks. It kept the American Army and the Red Ball moving from Normandy to the Elbe.

Charles Stevenson vividly remembered the importance of the jerrican. His unit was charged with filling them with gasoline, delivering them to combat units, and picking them up after they had been discarded by American troops.[1] Stevenson's job started in England well before D-Day. His unit, the 3858th QM Gas Supply Company, was stationed on the grounds of Sultram House, a rambling Georgian manor in Devonshire. For months prior to D-Day, the men of the 3858th unloaded and stacked thousands of jerricans on the estate grounds that were situated astride the Plym River before it empties into the English Channel at Plymouth.

The Germans might have known the importance of Stevenson's job because Sultram House was targeted during a Luftwaffe air raid. The manor suffered severe damage, but the stacks of loaded jerricans were unscathed.

151

In late May 1944, the roads around Plymouth were filled with tanks, half-tracks, trucks, jeeps, and armies of men. Lines of troops and vehicles from the 4th and 29th Infantry Divisions stretched between 15 and 20 miles back from the sea on the narrow English lanes into the lush and green Devon hills. Other units arrived from bivouac areas around towns and villages with such names as Ashburton and Tavistock. The men and vehicles were part of the massive military force lining up for the invasion of France.

The 3858th's job was to top off the gas tanks of the assembled vehicles in its sector. Stevenson's troops rode their trucks up and down the middle of the narrow lanes, widened two feet on either side to accommodate the large military vehicles, and handed out jerricans filled with gas to the tankers and truckers. As D-Day approached, the men even drove onto LSTs tied up in port to top off tanks in vehicles that soon would be in battle. Some trucks from the 3858th scooted off the LSTs just as the huge bow doors were closing and the vessels prepared for sea.

After the invasion force departed the English ports for Normandy, the fields of Devon and other English shires were littered with thousands of discarded jerricans. It was Stevenson's job to see that those in his sector were retrieved, cleaned, and refilled with gas before being sent to the continent.

The 3858th was shipped to France in late July 1944, where much of its work involved redistributing jerricans that were filled from an undersea pipeline laid from England to France by the Allies. Red Ball Jimmies then fanned out from the decanting stations across northern France to deliver them to the First and Third Armies. The need for gas was so great that the Army even turned to flatbed semitrailers and huge Sherman tank transporters to carry loads of the cans to the front. Tanker trucks, with a 2,000-gallon capacity, would have been a more economical way to transport gasoline, but the Army never had enough of these trucks. Besides, the jerrican was a convenient package that was easily carried.

The supply began to dwindle during the late summer of 1944, which touched off a crisis with strategic implications. Without jerricans, the Allies could not advance. The Army had accumulated a stock of more than 12 million in England prior to the invasion, but even this supply was considered inadequate. Army planners projected a need of 800,000 new cans a month and ordered 4½ million from British manufacturers to be supplied by the end of 1944.[2]

If military planners regarded jerricans as indispensable, so did the GIs. They used them in a thousand ways. Empty cans became chairs and tables, and walkways were constructed in bivouac areas by turning the cans on their sides in the mud and using them like giant bricks.

Air forces also used the containers. Large stocks of aviation gas were being delivered to air bases on the continent in jerricans. The U.S. Army Air Force (USAAF) had originally agreed to turn over several million jerricans to the ground forces once they had been emptied, but it kept them filled with aviation fuel as a static reserve.

Jerricans littered the wake of the American advance across France, through the Low Countries, and into Germany. Hundreds of thousands more were abandoned in dumps. To the American GI, they were an expendable item of war, bulky and a nuisance. It was easier to abandon them in the heat of the pursuit than to round them up and ship them back to depots to be refilled.[3]

By mid-October 1944, some 3,500,000 jerricans were unaccounted for and replacements had to be found immediately. Production levels, although increased, were insufficient to replace all of the lost cans. Recently liberated French production facilities were put on line with the expectation that 9 million more cans would be produced by the end of 1945. The Belgians also were contracted to produce another 2 million. By late 1944, the number of new cans needed to defeat the Germans was estimated to be 1,300,000 monthly.

In addition to arranging for the manufacture of new cans, the Army initiated a novel program to retrieve discarded jerricans by calling on the civilian population of France to turn in as many as they could find. Rewards were offered for each one returned to Allied hands.

The program also involved the French Ministry of Education, which appealed to French schoolchildren to round up lost cans. Prizes were given for the most cans returned, as were certificates of merit for a job well done. It was a successful endeavor. By the end of the campaign, the children of France had returned more than a million jerricans to Allied depots.

Just days before Germany surrendered on 8 May 1945, the Army was still scrounging for cans. Sgt. Frank Buergler, with the 94th Infantry Division, helped to retrieve German jerricans discarded by the retreating Wehrmacht. They were collected, filled, and sent out to American units. Buergler said that stretches of the German autobahn were turned into runways for jerrican-laden C-47s. The planes landed on the autobahn, unloaded gas-filled cans, and took off with empties.[4]

By the spring of 1945, as thousands of containers were wearing out from excessive use, the Army estimated that 50 percent of the entire stock would have to be replaced if the war lasted beyond June.

There is irony in the fact that the jerrican played such a prominent role in winning the war. It was a German design—hence its name—and was first encountered by the Americans in North Africa. Veteran British Eighth Army troops, who had fought Rommel's Afrika Korps for more than a year before the Americans arrived, had learned of the can's sturdiness and had given it its nickname. It was slimmer than the more squarish American gas containers, called "flimsies," that were fabricated from thin sheet metal and lived up to their name by frequently puncturing during transport. Ships carrying flimsies into North Africa would sometimes arrive in port with more than a foot of gasoline sloshing around in the hold. One ship was reported to have exploded because of leaking flimsies, and the Army estimated that it could lose 40–60 percent of the gasoline transported in these containers.

The jerrican was also easier to use. The nozzle was on the side, which facilitated the decanting of gasoline into recessed gas tank pipes.

When Rommel's army surrendered in Tunis in 1943, the Americans acquired large stocks of the German gas cans and soon adopted the superior design for their own gas containers. At first, the new American jerricans were called Ameri-cans, but the name never stuck. Forever after, it was the jerrican.[5]

TWENTY

EXHAUSTED JIMMIES

In November 1944, more than fifteen thousand broken-down American trucks in the ETO awaited repairs. By January 1945, as many as thirty-three thousand were out of service, and the Army estimated that another thirty-five thousand would be sidelined by March.[1] The trucks were in such poor condition that they were fodder for jokes. Cartoonist Bill Mauldin made light of the plague of wrecked Jimmies in a cartoon that depicted two soldiers exploring smashed-up vehicles in an Army salvage yard. One says to the other: "I'll be derned. Here's one what waz wrecked in combat."[2]

I Company's trucks had been driven 259,009 miles in August, with 53,725 miles logged between 6 and 13 August. The average weekly mileage accumulation for I Company trucks between 1 August and 24 September was 28,556, or 4,079 per day—excessive driving for trucks not designed for sustained long-haul operations.[3]

So many trucks were out of service in mid-September that the Army initiated a program of swapping Red Ball trucks for better-maintained vehicles from nonessential units. But good trucks soon became bad trucks once on the Red Ball, and units that were forced to turn over their vehicles were given derelicts in return. "You got somebody else's garbage in place of your well-maintained equipment," Charles Stevenson said.[4] His unit lost fifteen trucks to the Red Ball from 19 October to 18 December.

The men of C and I Companies, and all truckers, were expected to care for their trucks in the same way that cavalrymen had been expected to care for their horses. Preventive maintenance programs on the Red Ball, however, were often ignored, and the neglect shortened the useful lifespan of the vehicles.

Commanders did little to ensure that vehicles were properly maintained because the paramount objective of the Red Ball was to rush urgently needed supplies to the front. When a truck broke down, it was assumed that it could be repaired or replaced. This attitude became quasi-official Army policy as more and more Jimmies were assigned to the Red Ball.

The Army recognized, in one G-4 report, that disregard for proper maintenance "had been accepted in advance as necessary concomitants to the frantic if ordered haste demanded of the situation which tactical developments had thrown into the lap of COMZ." The history added:

> It must also be noted, however, that it had not been anticipated the strain on personnel and on equipment would last so long. It was believed that if the drive could be kept going there was a good chance of the war being won in a matter of a few weeks. The stake was worth a gamble. COMZ got in the game for all it was worth. Each time the armies raised the pot by another push ahead COMZ somehow dug from its pockets the wherewithal to meet the challenge.
>
> One example was the definite, though unwritten, decision not to ignore maintenance but to minimize it, to let equipment go to rack and ruin if by so doing the word "Finis" could be written to the war.[5]

Driver fatigue also contributed to poor maintenance. Truckers were at the wheel for such long periods that they had neither the time nor the energy to carry out even basic preventive maintenance work. Round-trips often required forty-eight to sixty-five hours of constant running, and drivers became so exhausted that they sometimes sabotaged their vehicles for a few hours of rest.

One tow truck operator on the Red Ball pulled alongside a stalled Jimmy and found that the driver had removed the spark plugs and points. The Army was aware that sabotage was a considerable problem and noted, in one G-4 report, "many instances of tampering with wiring, shorting of ignition systems, smashing of distributors, and similar bits of sabotage committed for the purpose of forcing the vehicle to fall out of the column."[6]

The Army even blamed press coverage of the Red Ball for the sorry state of its trucks:

> The tendency was to give a heroic cast to the men on the job. This, while stimulating to morale, had other effects not so satisfactory. There is little doubt that all this recognition went to the heads of Red Ball personnel, officers and men alike. . . .
>
> The Red Ball has been ballyhooed so much that drivers and convoy commanders have considered abuse of equipment justified in order to "win the war." This has led to overloading and overspeeding."[7]

The report referred particularly to blacks on the Red Ball and alluded that they, in particular, were influenced by the press reports. "It would have been amazing had it not [gone to their heads] especially considering the large proportion of drivers on the Red Ball who were Negroes and hence more than ordinarily responsive to expressions and marks of approval from high sources."[8]

The Army noted that although maintenance was poor on the Red Ball, the lack of proper vehicle care was not isolated to this operation alone or even to military operations in World War II. Prewar studies noted the lack of preventive care that American troops gave to their vehicles. Thompson and Mayo reported:

> In the fall of 1941 a spot check of about one-third of the motor vehicles of five divisions, made by a group of mechanics under the control of the Inspector General, showed that forty-seven percent of the vehicles were improperly lubricated, fifty

percent had distributors loose or dirty and points badly burned, forty-nine percent had loose steering gear housings, fifty-three percent had under inflated tires, twenty-three percent had improper wheel alignment, thirty-six percent had dry batteries and thirty-seven percent had tires that were badly worn, cupped, and improperly mounted. There was no reason to believe that this discovery did not represent average conditions throughout the Army; and it was plain that the conditions were mainly the fault of careless drivers.[9]

The conditions that prevailed in 1941 continued throughout the war. Thompson and Mayo noted that truck maintenance in general was so poor during the war that "in one theater a supply train carrying ammunition, rations, fuel, and lubricants to a regiment about to launch an offensive literally fell apart, with more than fifty percent of the trucks on deadline [broken down]. . . . " In this instance, however, it was pointed out that the problem was not only improper maintenance "but also because the corps permitted the trucks to run twenty-four hours a day for weeks without any time out for unkeep."[10]

The Chief of Ordnance, who was responsible for repair work on the trucks in the ETO, recommended that the Army set up a "line" servicing organization, or what was called the "40 and 8 system," in which forty trucks were on the road while eight were being repaired. Each vehicle would undergo a maintenance check after completing a round-trip to and from a forward depot, but the plan meant sidelining trucks that were still running and capable of transporting supplies. It might be practical under normal circumstance but not on the Red Ball where every truck still operating was needed.

The 40 and 8 system would also mean that large numbers of trucks that traveled alone or in small groups or on special assignment for days at a time would miss their servicing dates.

Another maintenance suggestion was for a centralized station to which all trucks would report. The G-4 history noted:

The plan was based on 7,000 vehicles on the Red Ball and a trip turn-around of three days, so that 2,300 vehicles a day would require servicing. It envisaged giving first and second echelon maintenance and partial 6,000-mile servicing. Third and fourth echelon work would be done by Ordnance automotive maintenance units in adjoining installations. Changing drivers and refueling would take place at the service station. Bivouac areas would be located near the station, but no vehicles would enter them. The whole scheme was designed to approximate commercial practices, but adapted to military needs.[11]

This plan was never implemented because it was assumed that the Red Ball was still a temporary organization.[12]

The poor condition of the Army's Jimmies was compounded by a worldwide shortage of spare parts.

"We can't get spare parts," lamented John Axselle, a driver with the 146th QM Truck Company, during an interview on the U.S. Army Radio Service to explain the Red Ball to the troops in Europe. His complaints were echoed at the highest levels. Col. Ward E. Becker, an ordnance officer with service in North Africa and the Pacific Theater, wrote a colleague about the consequences of not having an adequate supply of truck parts for the trucks:

> Our chief headache continues to be shortage of fast moving maintenance parts for wheeled vehicles. . . . Our vehicles have received tortuous treatment. . . .
>
> In general, a 2½ ton truck engine requires 4th echelon rebuild in 10,000 miles, due largely to the lack of parts with which to properly take care of 2nd and 3rd echelon maintenance. Another reason, however, is lack of maintenance discipline. . . . We have rear axles for GMC trucks "running out of our ears" but zero stocks of point sets, main bearing kits, carburetor repair kits, overhaul gasket sets, spark plugs, oil filters, etc. . . . In many units from 50–75 percent of the vehicles require . . . repairs which cannot be made due to lack of parts.

> Pardon my lengthy cry on your shoulder. If you could see our pathetic array of deadlined trucks, I really believe that you would feel my official tears are justified.[13]

Spare parts were so scarce for trucks and tanks that Patton dispatched quartermaster teams to scavenge junk yards for transfer cases, steering assemblies, and other critical parts. Col. Thomas H. Nixon, Third Army ordnance officer, sent searchers all the way back to depots around Cherbourg. Even as late as mid-December 1944, more than half of all automotive supplies remained in Normandy and Brittany because priority was given to ammunition, food, and gasoline for shipment to the front.

When parts were not available, Nixon employed French firms to make them or had them made in Army shops. The Americans were inventive. One shop fabricated a tool for straightening bent axles and for adapting British axles to American vehicles. Another shop built a magnetic road sweep to clear the metal shards that littered the Red Ball Highway.[14]

In a postmortem Army report, Thompson and Mayo noted:

> As far as Ordnance history is concerned, it is no exaggeration to say that spare parts, particularly for trucks and tanks, posed one of the most important and persistent problems of the whole war. In Africa, General Rommel's success in recovering from defeats was often ascribed to the fact that he was well equipped with parts and had a competent maintenance organization while the British were less well off. "When I die," a high-ranking British Ordnance officer once remarked, 'spare parts,' will be written across my heart."[15]

Ernie Pyle also weighed in on the problem:

> This is not a war of ammunition, tanks, guns, and trucks alone. It is as much a war of replenishing spare parts to keep them in combat as it is a war of major equipment. . . . The gasket that leaks, the fan belt that breaks, the nut that is lost . . . will delay

GI Joe on the road to Berlin just as much as if he didn't have a vehicle in which to start."[16]

Thompson and Mayo noted that spare parts for vehicles "were numbered in the hundreds of thousands, and the quantity of some, like spark plugs and tires, ran into the millions." The logistics of getting all these items to the exact point where they were needed was almost overwhelming. "They ranged in size from delicate springs weighing a fraction of an ounce to tank engines weighing more than half a ton. They had to be produced in huge quantities and also had to be named, numbered, packed and shipped to all corners of the globe."[17]

One of the greatest shortages was in replacement tires, particularly for Red Ball trucks. In early October 1944, the Transportation Corps had reported a shortage of 180,236 tires of all types, but the total number of spare tires available on the continent and in Great Britain was less than 50,000.[18]

Military truck tires had a life expectancy of about 12,000 miles, but trucks could accumulate this much mileage on the Red Ball in a few weeks. Mileage alone did not wear out tires. They were battered by potholes, sliced and punctured by debris lying on the roads, weakened by low pressure, and even incinerated by friction. According to a G-4 report, 65 percent of all tires ruined on the Red Ball were inadvertently damaged or destroyed by the drivers themselves.[19]

Tires were also destroyed by excessive weight and underinflation. Robert Emerick was stopped by MPs for carrying too heavy a load in his 2½-ton truck. Such warnings, however, were almost always ignored. On the next assignment, Emerick helped to carry an evacuation hospital closer to the front lines. "That tent canvas is about the heaviest and densest load you can carry, and we had Jimmies piled full clear up to just above the sideboards. It was between 8 and 10 tons on the trucks and they got to rockin' and rollin' a little bit because it was top heavy."[20]

Sometimes a tire went flat while on the run, particularly with heavy loads, but convoys did not stop if the flat was on the rear

and a good tire remained on the dual wheel mount and the vehicle could still roll. This meant, however, that the good tire was
even more taxed under the heavy loads, bad roads, and high
speeds. Many trucks carried no spares so when a lone front tire
went flat the driver had no alternative but to keep driving on the
rim, and the tire was destroyed before the vehicle arrived at the
nearest maintenance depot. Tires driven while flat would sometimes overheat and burst into flame, forcing trucks and convoys
to pull over to extinguish the fire before it consumed truck and
cargo.[21]

Tire repair shops were hastily established in the liberated areas,
but there were not enough of these facilities to keep pace with the
attrition on the Red Ball. In one instance, 39,835 tires awaited
repair, but facilities to fix only 2,953 tires were available.

The 12th Army Group was seriously concerned about the tire
shortage, particularly when COMZ predicted in September 1944
that, by January 1945, the Army would suffer a deficit of some
250,000 tires. In desperation, the Chief of Transportation began
deadlining all 1-ton trailers and one thousand vehicles for lack of
tires.[22]

Quartermaster units did whatever they could to keep the
trucks rolling. They stripped tires from trailers in nonessential
units, scavenged tires from 37-mm gun carriages and even enemy
vehicles, and made do with recapped and reconstituted tires that
were barely adequate.

Charles Stevenson was shocked by the terrible quality of the
retreaded and rebuilt tires that his unit received during the
shortage. On one move forward on the Red Ball Highway, his
trucks experienced a series of flat tires during the first hour of
travel. Stevenson said:

We weren't running over anything, they were just bad tires. You
could see where the ration cans cut into the rubber. Sometimes
you could see the old bullet holes that had been plugged. These
weren't steel-belted tires. They were plain, old rubber tires with
an inner tube and they'd try to patch them as best they could.

But they had bumps in them and all kinds of sticky tape and stuff. They did everything they could but it wasn't too swift.[23]

The Army blamed the overall spare parts problem on the fact that the truck, a new innovation in warfare, was far more complex than anyone realized. Thompson and Mayo noted of the truck, "It usually breaks down one part at a time. And the whole vehicle may be immobilized for lack of that one part, whether it be a simple item like a cracked spark plug or something more intricate like a burned out bearing."[24]

Ordnance personnel had no long-term maintenance data relating to the durability of trucks, nor had anyone in the Army ever expected trucks to log hundreds of thousands of miles, often during combat conditions, over the battered roads of the European Theater.

Thompson and Mayo noted that there were few complaints about parts shortages and maintenance for "shooting ordnance"— rifles, machine guns, and artillery pieces. The Army attributed this to the fact that "ordnance experience with rifles and artillery weapons ran back for over one hundred years, and with machine guns about half that time. Decades of development work, combined with long experience in field maintenance, had built up a solid backlog of maintenance data, including fairly exact knowledge of what replacement parts would be needed."[25]

Thompson and Mayo quoted one Army study: "When unit commanders realize that a motor vehicle is a fighting weapon, the greater part of the transport problems will be solved."[26]

Somehow, the trucks in the ETO continued to roll all the way to the Elbe without ever being adequately maintained. Only the war's end in May 1945 finally gave trucks and drivers their needed respite.

TWENTY-ONE

TRAINS AND PLANES

Because the strains on Red Ball trucks were mounting, the Army proposed in mid-September that the Red Ball east of Paris be terminated by 20 October 1944 and that all long-haul cargoes normally carried by truck be transferred to the railroads. Red Ball vehicles would be used primarily to transport supplies to and from railheads on short-haul trips. The Army's Military Railway Service was up and running, and enough track had been repaired east of Paris for trains to carry up to 4,000 tons of supplies daily to the First and Third Armies.

The Army even began using truck-to-rail transfer points in the Paris area and in eastern France as U.S. forces closed on the German frontier. This was welcome news for Red Ball commanders. The G-4 history of the Red Ball quoted one COMZ officer as saying at the time that "the rails taking over soon may just save the situation, as remedial action [on trucks] cannot wait more than two more weeks."[1]

Rail transfer points for Red Ball supplies were established in the Paris area at La Courneuve for First Army supplies and at Vincennes-Fontenay for Third Army supplies. Farther east, such units as the 62d QM Base Depot set up truck-rail transfer stations closer to the front. The 62d established operations at Sommesous, about 90 miles east of Paris, where its principal mission was to unload supplies from Red Ball trucks and reload them on trains for shipment to the Third and Ninth Armies.

The Sommesous transfer point, however, was soon left behind as the Third Army pushed forward, and the 62d opened another transfer point at Lerouville, another 90 miles farther east.[2]

Despite the best efforts to move supplies by rail, the Army quickly learned that the truck was still indispensable, and the plans to terminate the Red Ball completely were dropped. Trains did not have the flexibility needed in a war of maneuver, and time was being lost in transferring materiel from truck to train and train to truck. Training French workers to properly load rail cars with military cargo in the Paris region also proved difficult. The workers paid no attention to instructions from U.S. military personnel, particularly when handling ammunition and explosives, and there were not enough U.S. supervisors to check each railcar before it was shipped.

Nevertheless, work on repairing the railroads continued apace in the belief that, during a prolonged war, trains would carry the bulk of materiel to the front. Many engineering units were diverted from highway to railroad work, particularly after the precipitous German retreat had helped to preserve the main roads in eastern France that had escaped systematic air attacks like those that destroyed much of the road network in the Normandy area. In consequence, roadwork east of Paris consisted mainly of filling potholes or rebuilding bridges that the Germans had blown as they fell back.

The mission of the 341st Engineer Regiment reflected the change in work priorities:

> During the later part of August, as the First and Third Armies were making their spectacular and furious drive eastward through France and Paris and beyond, it became apparent that the need for road construction engineers was less important than the need for railroad engineers to put the transportation system in a working order as soon as possible. . . . The fact that the Regiment had had more than two years' experience in road and bridge building and repair, both on the Alaska Highway and on the continent, but had had practically no experience in railroad work didn't faze the officers and men."[3]

As a result, the job of road construction in much of France was turned over to French civilian workers and German POWs.

During the later stages of the pursuit, the Army began delivering materiel to combat units by air whenever possible. The concept of air supply was in its infancy in the ETO during 1944. C-47s had dropped food and ammunition to various units during the days and weeks after D-Day. In one instance, these twin-engine workhorses dropped supplies to an antiaircraft artillery unit stranded by bad weather on the Îles Saint-Marcouf off Utah Beach. In another situation, planes delivered food, ammunition, and medicines to an infantry battalion cut off during the German counterattacks at Mortain in early August.

A smooth working concept for air supply, however, never had been actually tested. There were too few cargo planes available, not enough truck capacity available for loading and unloading the planes when they landed, and inadequate landing facilities on the continent to handle a steady stream of planes bringing in supplies. The Allies even turned to B-17s and B-24s to ferry cargo to the continent but these added little to the effort.[4]

To make matters worse, the high command was putting together Operation Market Garden, which required hundreds of C-47s to prepare and train for the airborne operation. When Paris was liberated, the Allies diverted even more C-47s to deliver some 2,400 tons of supplies each day, which left little capacity to supply combat troops.

Air shipments to forward areas reached their peak on 26 and 27 August, when deliveries totaled nearly 2,900 tons for the two days. They declined precipitately after 29 August when the C-47s withdrew for service in Operation Market Garden and air delivery was conducted by some one hundred converted bombers. Without the C-47s, the airlift failed to meet the needs of both the Army and the people of Paris.[5]

According to historian Roland Ruppenthal, "From August 19, when the airlift began, to the end of the pursuit in mid-September, American transport planes carried a total of 20,000 tons to Twelfth Army Group. This is in stark contrast to the tonnage carried on the Red Ball. During the same period the Red Ball carried some 135,000 tons to First and Third Armies. In the end the airlift did not measure up to expectations, and it fell far short of the early goal of 3,000 tons per day."[6]

The truck remained the essential vehicle of delivery in the ETO, and the Red Ball Express still carried the bulk of supplies to the advancing armies. It would continue to be the workhorse of the Army throughout the remainder of the war in France, during the Battle of the Bulge, and in the final assault on Germany.

TWENTY-TWO

BUZZ BOMB
ALLEY

In late summer 1944, Red Ball troops faced a new threat not encountered in Normandy. The Germans were launching V-1 flying bombs and V-2 rockets by the thousands against civilian and military targets in Great Britain, Belgium, and northern France. The V-1 was the principal robot bomb used, but the silent, more devastating V-2 was also employed.

The V-1 sounded like a passing motorboat as it scooted over convoys and drew fire from antiaircraft guns along its path. Soldiers were often treated to fireworks displays of ack-ack and tracers crisscrossing the sky in the wake of a buzz bomb. Fighters also chased the robot bombs.

Two principal targets for the V-1 and V-2s on the continent were the vast American depots at Antwerp and Liège. The historian for the 3630th QM Truck Company wrote:

> However, undaunted, the convoys continued to roll into Liège's dumps and depots while German radio broadcasts openly boasted that their bombs had ruined these supply points or made them untenable. Truly enough, the bravery and determination of the American effort alone disproved this as the drivers sweated out exploding gas dumps and near misses from the hundreds of bombs falling around the installations.[1]

The 3611th QM Truck Company also experienced the V-1s and V-2s. An entry in the unit history recorded the danger:

Unit arrives in Antwerp. . . . Assignment becomes a life threatening experience. It continues daily until March 26, 1945. In the four month period hundreds of V-1 and V-2 rockets (1 ton war head) fall in Antwerp area. In spite of the continuous daily bombardment, Unit experiences no loss of life. Some injuries incurred but few came forward to receive medical aid.[2]

Depots were targeted wherever they existed. Six members of the 3597th QM Truck Company were killed in northern France when a V-2 rocket scored a direct hit on an ammunition dump from which company trucks were operating.

Cpl. George C. Nichols with the 3611th recalled the dangers of the robot bombs.

I was standing on the fender just getting ready to get in the cab when it (a V-1) went off. It was about a hundred yards away and killed a lot of civilians. You could see wood and everything flying high in the air. They took me to an aid station but I didn't stay there long. As long as you don't get caught in the ring of concussion of the bombs you are OK. One person can be two hundred yards away and get killed, another the same distance away on the other side will be safe.[3]

Luftwaffe planes still threatened Red Ball vehicles and could strike suddenly from the sky, particularly as the Americans closed on Germany. When the advance quickened in late August and early September, more and more trucks drove through the night with lights ablaze, as the drivers chanced that German fighters were too few to be a threat. This practice sometimes proved dangerous. James Chappelle heard the rattle of machine-gun fire as German fighters swept over a C Company convoy. The planes came and went before the men could react, and the trucks continued on without incident. No one had been hit.[4]

Merle Gutherie, who had delivered papers to Eisenhower's mother in Abilene, Kansas, was in a convoy strafed by German planes. His truck carried a .50-caliber machine gun in a ring above the cab, and Gutherie relished the challenge of taking on a Nazi fighter. It reminded him of his duck-hunting days back home. "I jumped up and four of us started shooting at them. I'd shot a lot of ducks as a kid so I knew how to lead them with the tracers. We got one of them because he came down in a plume of smoke."[5]

The historian of the 283d Field Artillery Battalion wrote about the excitement and dangers that lurked from the air as volunteer drivers approached Liège. As their TNT-laden convoy slowly drove through the blacked out city, "flares with their cold, revealing glare gave us the first intimation that a German plane was stalking us." Nearby, 90-mm antiaircraft guns and .50-caliber machine guns opened up and brought a German plane down in flames.[6]

Charles Weko, a lieutenant with the 6660th QM Truck Company, thought of home and Christmas during the heady days of the pursuit. Without warning, the Luftwaffe jumped the volunteer unit. Enemy bullets, tearing into the convoy, sounded like "stones being hurled against corrugated metal." At first, Weko was puzzled, then terrified, as he heard the brittle clatter of machine guns from strafing Luftwaffe fighters.

"Everyone stopped their machines and ran like deer." Weko jumped from his truck and threw himself into a ditch. All along the road, Red Ball drivers abandoned their vehicles and scattered into nearby fields.[7]

Mines remained a constant danger. A group from the 894th watched in horror as a farmer touched off a land mine while plowing his fields near their bivouac area. The man lost a leg and his son in the blast.

Mine-detecting engineers were a common sight along the road shoulders, as were signs warning the truckers to steer to the middle of the highway in areas where the shoulders had not been properly cleared.

As a precaution, truckers sometimes packed the floorboards of their vehicles with sandbags to absorb the blast if they ran over a mine, but this protection was often illusory. T/4 Richard W. Gardner drove over a mine and was blown from the vehicle. He catapulted 30 feet into the air before landing, unscathed, in the bed of a nearby Jimmy.[8]

As the Third Army rolled through eastern France, truckers faced threats from pro-German inhabitants in the regions of Alsace and Lorraine along the Franco-German border. The French and Germans had long fought over their sovereignty. In 1940, following the fall of France, Germany controlled Alsace and Lorraine. Hitler moved thousands of die-hard Nazis into the area and expelled some thirty-five thousand French nationals.

When the Red Ball followed the Third Army into Alsace and Lorraine, there was little cheering for the conquering Americans. They encountered sullen hostility and began to experience acts of espionage and sabotage.[9]

As in Normandy, truckers still faced pockets of German troops that had been bypassed by Allied forces. The 146th moved forward in September, and historian Bass noted that "a lot of places still had enemy stragglers who would shoot at MPs and also at us at times."[10]

I Company ran into a group of German soldiers near the German frontier. Corporal Brice noted in his history:

> Early last night the company was awakened by extensive gun fire. This took on the aspect of a pitched battle. Shots were fired back and forth and became so protracted that we were all assembled in the neighborhood of the mess truck under the leadership of Technical Sergeant Robert Brown. He had machine guns set up, for our protection. By the time this was done the fire had become sporadic and was no longer directed towards us. Corporal Oliver Donaldson assumed command of a gun in our area, but no action was necessary. Later in the morning Sergeant Brown and Corporal Eulah Coe went on patrol through the deep woods from whence the shots had come. They reached an antiaircraft gun position in a field near the outskirts of the woods, and the gunners showed them the

bodies of two Germans they had shot in the woods. Four others had escaped they said, and were still at large. Continuing on they found the body of another German.[11]

The war still raged, and the need to haul supplies to the front was as urgent as ever. The Americans were stopped at the German frontier, and the struggle to dislodge the Germans consumed vast quantities of ammunition. Truck companies continued to drive all day and all night with only cat eyes to guide them over the strange roads. In late September and early October, the urgency of their mission was evident from the distant rumble of artillery from American guns besieging the Siegfried Line. The truck drivers were often guided by the amber glow on the northern horizon that was the reflection of fires consuming Aachen and other towns and cities on the frontiers of Germany.

TWENTY-THREE

JOINING THE INFANTRY

By December 1944, the policy of denying blacks the right to fight in integrated combat units came back to haunt the nation. As the American Army approached its authorized strength of 7,770,000 men and engaged the enemy on a broad front in the ETO, the number of casualties rose dramatically. The Joint Chiefs of Staff had restricted the size of the Army to 7,770,000 men in accordance with a strategic plan to provide adequate manpower for a 4,000,000-man Navy and a skilled civilian workforce to produce the weapons needed to defeat the Axis powers.

From D-Day to V-E Day, American losses in the ETO totaled 586,628, including 135,576 dead.[1] The Battle of the Bulge alone cost the American Army 80,000 casualties.[2] The nation's manpower reserves dwindled as the pool of eligible men declined. By late 1944, the Army's new divisions consisted largely of eighteen-year-olds. All of the new infantrymen were white.

Whites who held such rear echelon positions as clerks and cooks were pressed into combat units and sent into the lines. Because of a long-standing army policy of segregation, however, blacks could not be similarly impressed into infantry units. General Lee, the commander of COMZ, recognized that the large number of black troops under his command constituted a considerable source of untapped manpower that could be employed in the infantry. In a radical move that initiated integration in the army, and that had the approval and support of

Gen. Eisenhower, Lee asked for infantry volunteers among his black service troops.

"Combat officers were coming around asking [black] truckers to volunteer for infantry duty at the Bulge," Chester Jones said. "My opinion was: they said I didn't have sense enough to be a combat soldier stateside—well if I didn't have it then I damned sure didn't have it in their emergency."[3]

Brig. Gen. Benjamin Davis, the highest-ranking black officer in the military at that time, visited C Company. Davis had risen through the ranks, and he was the father of Col. Benjamin Davis, commander of the 332d Fighter Group. "Davis wanted us to contribute to our country and came to entice us to join the infantry. Volunteer!! The Infantry!! You Crazy!!" Chappelle said.[4] Chappelle's response reflected the feelings of some of the men.

"The way I felt about it was what's the use of going out and fighting when you're a second class citizen. What good is that?" James Rookard said.[5]

To the majority of the African Americans on the Red Ball, appeals to their patriotism had a hollow ring. They drove trucks because their Army and country believed that they were not qualified for combat roles. To this day, many aging African Americans are outraged by the treatment and attitudes to which they were subjected during World War II. Their feelings, then and now, might be expressed as they were back then by a black soldier to Lt. Col. John H. Sherman, who commanded black troops during the war:

> 'How come white folks is fightin' Hitler for treatin' the Jews just like they treat us?' I could find no adequate answer in any Army regulation or textbook. . . . Any officer who lives their life with them, eating in the same mess, sleeping in the same area, attending their chapel, visiting their dayrooms, buying in their exchanges, and showing interest in their sports and social activities, soon finds that these men are passionately eager for pride, self-respect and friends to whom they can give trust and loyalty.

Those are the things Negroes will work for, eagerly fight for, gladly die for. I know. I have seen them do all three.[6]

The call for black volunteers produced some results. According to historian Lee, "By February [1945], 4,562 Negro troops had volunteered, many of the non-commissioned officers among them taking reductions in rank to do so. The first 2,800 reported to the Ground Forces Reinforcement Command in January and early February. . . . "[7] These men completed a course of instruction and were formed into thirty-seven newly established rifle platoons. Led by a white lieutenant or sergeant, each unit totaled some sixty men, about 50 percent over normal strength to provide a ready source of replacements for battle casualties.[8]

The inclusion of blacks in white combat formations did not produce shoulder-to-shoulder integration. The blacks were assigned to white companies by platoons, rather than as individual replacements. Thus, the Army still remained segregated. The military had started down the road to complete integration, however, particularly as the program yielded exceptional marks for the black combat troops. After-action reports submitted by 84 percent of the white officers and 81 percent of the sergeants who commanded the black volunteers indicated that the volunteers had done "very well" in combat and had performed as well as whites. White and black troops had also operated without the usual friction between the two races.

One infantry battalion commander gave the black volunteers under his command his highest recommendation. According to historian Lee, he reported:

I know I did not receive a superior representation of the colored race. . . . I do know, however, that in courage, coolness, dependability and pride, they are on a par with any white troops I have ever had occasion to work with. In addition, they were, during combat, possessed with a fierce desire to meet with and kill the enemy, the equal of which I have never witnessed in white troops.[9]

It frustrated many blacks that whites saw them as lacking in fortitude. Imbued with stories about their own shortcomings, blacks were sometimes startled to see whites throwing down their weapons and running from the enemy. Chester Jones said that, while hauling white infantrymen out of harm's way during the Battle of the Bulge, "it struck me as strange they were leaving the scene where their kind of action was."[10]

Horace Evans was with the 761st Tank Battalion, one of the few all-black combat units to fight in the ETO. He recounted an experience of fighting alongside white troops:

> I recall an incident where white soldiers of the 87th Infantry that were fighting with our tanks for cover could have been called cowards. We had to plead with them, coax them, put their packs on their backs, beg them to go on with their outfit. They could be shot for desertion, we pointed out, because they were determined they were through fighting. They just weren't going to fight anymore and they were in tears. I don't ever recall a black soldier in my outfit crying. I witnessed a lot of cussin', but not crying.[11]

Another soldier in the same unit, Horace Jones, recounted a time when he saw a white soldier wound himself rather than face battle:

> A white officer ran down the road to where his troops sat or sprawled in various positions. He told them to get on their feet, we were moving up. As the captain passed on, this white soldier, obviously a hillbilly, said, "By God if I'm going," raised his foot, took his M1 rifle and put a bullet through it. . . . And that was a whitey and I witnessed that with my own eyes.[12]

If there was any consolation for black troops serving on the continent, it was that the racism was somewhat muted compared to that in England and the United States because whites were preoccupied with fighting Germans. Also, the African Americans were performing valuable duties, and some whites, at least, recognized the black contribution.

There were hints of change to come. An editorial in the military newspaper *Stars and Stripes* addressed the problems of race in an editorial titled, "Let's Set the Post War Pattern":

> About one in every 10 in this man's army is a Negro. Wherever you go, from the beaches to the front you'll see these lads doing their stuff, which leads up to the story of three GIs, white boys who were caught on the road one night with the gas needle angling towards zero. They made several bids to refill without success until they pulled into an orchard where a Negro medic outfit was dug in for the night. Piled in neat stacks under a tree were about 30 cans, all empty, empty that is except for a few drops that always get stuck inside the neck of a GI can. These Negro GIs came out of the holes and tilted the empties into one can. By the time thirty cans were wrung dry there was enough gas in the jeep to get to the next dump. "Don't mention it" is what the Negro sergeant said as the GIs resumed their journey. The decent things Joes do for each other ought to be mentioned. They ought to make things a little bit easier when we all go back home.[13]

Nevertheless, racism remained a serious problem. Chester Jones said that a Red Cross center that opened in Cherbourg shortly after the fighting ended was off limits to black soldiers until a white chaplain interceded. Jones had run into off-limits signs at Red Cross centers in Great Britain.[14]

Rookard found prejudice running so deep that it could be difficult sometimes to find a place to eat on the Red Ball Highway. At one rest area, he asked for a mess kit, and a group of white soldiers objected to Rookard's using borrowed utensils. "One of them got real mad but I used it anyway. I was hungry and I couldn't eat out of my hands," he said.[15]

Racial conflict always seemed to erupt when white women were involved. Chester Jones visited a bar in Paris in which the only other patrons were prostitutes. He had a drink with one of them while his buddy went upstairs with another. Two drunken white soldiers entered, and one was offended because Jones was sitting with a white woman. "You black sons-of-bitches don't sit with white women at home, and I'll be damned if you'll do it here while I'm around," he said. The white soldier drew a 45-caliber pistol and marched Jones outside with the gun shoved into his back. Jones was surprised when the white soldier did not shoot him but only warned him to stay away from the bar.[16]

Charles Weko literally saved his platoon sergeant's neck while he was stationed in France. The sergeant, named Elmer, regularly took clothing and linen to a laundry operated by several French-women, and he made the mistake of having an affair with one of the women who was also claimed by a white American officer.

"The white officer found out, and he had Elmer up for rape," Weko recounted. "That was a hell of a thing. I had to go talk to the general to get him back."[17]

"About race prejudice," said Floyd Jones, a master sergeant with the 578th Field Artillery Battalion in the ETO, "the Europeans in our line of march had no racial hangups. Those my group met were French, Belgians, and Germans. Now I ran into prejudice and discrimination in Europe, don't misunderstand me, but it was marked, 'Made in the United States.' Ole 'Mister Charlie' was there to make sure you never left home, so to speak."[18]

The Germans whom Jones encountered must not have been Nazis. They, of course, had a few "racial hang-ups." Nevertheless, the sting was still felt more than a half century after the war. As Rookard said, "Yes, I'm bitter about it, but I'm taking it in stride. Then, I was r-e-a-l angry."[19]

TWENTY-FOUR

THE FINAL DAYS

Success brought down the curtain on the Red Ball Express. By the fall of 1944, it had done its job. The Wehrmacht in France and in much of the Low Countries had been defeated. The channel ports had been captured. Antwerp was open, and supplies were being shipped to the vast depots at Liège and Verdun and to the front. The reconstruction of the French rail system and the creation of truck-to-rail transfer points meant that some materiel once sent by truck across France now could be transported by rail. Trucks no longer had to make the long journey back to the invasion beaches. The need for the Red Ball diminished daily.

From its peak performance when it transported 12,342 tons of supplies on 29 August, the Red Ball settled down to haul an average of 5,088 tons per day until 25 October when the loads dipped to an average of 2,711 tons daily. From then on, to the last day of the operation, tonnages declined. On 1 November, total tons carried on the Red Ball declined to 1,644 daily and seldom went above 2,000 tons thereafter.[1]

From a high-water mark when some 132 truck companies served on the Red Ball during the first week of September, only 5 companies were left by mid-November, Red Ball's last week. On average, some 83 truck companies served on the Red Ball during its eighty-one days of operation, with an average of 899 trucks operating on the highway on any given day.

The average length of a Red Ball road trip was 606 miles. The total number of tons carried on the Red Ball operation was 412,143. In all, the total ton miles transported by Red Ball trucks came to 121,873,929, for an average daily haul of 1,504,616 ton miles.[2]

The Red Ball undoubtedly would have remained in operation beyond 16 November 1944 had the First and Third Armies continued their advances into Germany before the winter of 1944–45. The G-4 history noted:

> A plan was laid on by G-4, COMZ whereby a large part of the Red Ball trucks would be bivouacked in the Namur, Belgium, and Verdun, France, areas, hauling supplies forward from the Reims-Soissons area to AdSec [Advanced Section, COMZ] dumps. The logic behind this move was that in event of a breakthrough on either side of the front, L of C [lines of communication] truck hauls would be possible at once merely by extending the lines and utilizing the same bivouac area and command.[3]

Had the plan been implemented, Red Ball trucks would have delivered 12,000 tons of supplies a day to the First Army 100 miles to the north and 6,000 tons daily to the Third Army 100 miles to the south. The railroads moved many of the supplies during the winter stalemate along the Siegfried Line, and plans for a continuation of the Red Ball were dropped except for the creation of forward bivouac areas for the trucks.[4]

Nevertheless, this plan was employed a month later during the Battle of the Bulge when the ghost of the Red Ball played a major role in defeating the German attack. Thousands of trucks were ready and available to transport hundreds of thousands of troops and tons of supplies to the battlefront.

Even after the Battle of the Bulge, the Red Ball never really died during the remainder of the war in the ETO. Red Ball set the stage for future express trucking lines that carried supplies to U.S. armies advancing across Germany to the Elbe River. Army commanders learned from Red Ball's shortcomings and adopted important changes. As the armies moved into Germany, they were supported by new and efficiently run express lines with such names as ABC and XYZ.

On 2 December, the Army published SOP No. 53, which listed many of Red Ball's shortcomings, particularly those pertaining to convoy operations "which had been so many and so glaring, and so often the subject of unfavorable remarks by inspecting officers." The Army realized that improved regulations would be necessary for the drive into Germany, where it was assumed that trucks would carry the bulk of supplies because the rail lines were in even worse shape than those in France prior to D-Day.[5]

The Army's G-4 history of the Red Ball noted the following items among the changes adopted for the new trucking lines:

Convoys must not be less than the standard platoon of 20 trucks.

The convoy commander must ride habitually at the rear of the convoy [to curtail straggling].

All convoys not clearly marked Red Ball will be checked at all TCPs for proper clearance.

Red Ball vehicles found in town, off the Red Ball route, will be checked, and, if not on official business, will be reported to the appropriate headquarters for disciplinary action.

Straggler vehicles, loaded or empty, will be apprehended by the military police and turned over to the nearest TCP, where a record will be prepared identifying the vehicles, their drivers, and the parent unit involved. The stragglers will be held at the TCP until they can be joined to convoys moving to the stragglers' authorized destination. On request of the Motor Transport Service, TCPs will make straggler vehicle records available.

If a disabled vehicle left beside the road is repaired, the driver will obtain from the Ordnance Maintenance Company a certificate showing the exact time the vehicle was undergoing service and the time it was released.

Where a vehicle has to be turned in to an Ordnance maintenance unit, the driver will remain with the vehicle until he obtains the properly documented receipt of a replacement vehicle by transfer.

If a driver is injured, or otherwise unable to stay with his vehicle, the convoy commander must see that it is left in charge of a qualified individual.

When a vehicle has to drop out of a convoy, the convoy commander will furnish the driver a written authorization to do so, including a statement of the controlling reason.

Motor Transport Service will arrange for company bivouacs to provide emergency gassing facilities and to assure convoys having sufficient fuel to carry out their missions.

No civilians may be carried on Red Ball vehicles.

Exceptions to one-way traffic rule, not requiring specific authorization by HQ COMZ, will be emergency vehicles such as fire-fighting equipment, ambulances, military police and ordnance patrols.

Diversion of truck companies, battalions, or groups from Red Ball operation will be made only on authority of HQ COMZ issued through COT [Chief of Transportation].

This SOP tying up ends which had hung loosely during the original Red Ball's life, goes far toward assuring that a new Red Ball will be as resultful as its famous predecessor and have fewer bugs in its system.[6]

On 1 October, General Eisenhower recognized the efforts of the men on the now famous Red Ball Express:

To: The Officers and Men of the Red Ball Highway.

1) In any war, there are two tremendous tasks. That of the combat troops is to fight the enemy. That of the supply troops is to furnish all the materiel to insure victory. The faster and farther the combat troops advance against the foe, the greater becomes the battle of supply.

2) The menace of the Atlantic has been conquered. Supplies are reaching the continent in increasing streams. But the battle

to get those supplies to the front becomes daily of mounting importance.

3) On the continent, the Red Ball Line is the lifeline between combat and supply. To it falls the tremendous task of getting vital supplies from ports and depots to the combat troops, when and where vital supplies are needed, materiel without which the Armies might fail.

4) To you the drivers and the mechanics and your officers, who keep the Red Ball vehicles constantly moving, I wish to express my deep appreciation. You are doing an excellent job.

5) But the struggle is not yet won, for the enemy still fights. So the Red Ball must continue the battle it is waging so well, with the knowledge that each truckload which goes through to the combat forces cannot help but bring victory.

Dwight D. Eisenhower
General, U.S. Army[7]

TWENTY-FIVE

VICTORY
IN THE BULGE

"The real hero of the Bulge was GI Joe, Combat GI Joe," historian Robert Leckie wrote in *Delivered from Evil*.[1]

The Battle of the Bulge was also victory and vindication for the truck and, indirectly, for the drivers of the old Red Ball Express who played major and equally decisive roles in the battle. By mid-December 1944, the efficient transport of infantry by truck was a critical factor in turning the tide of this battle in the Ardennes. According to General Bradley, "He [Hitler] had forgotten that this time he was opposed [in the bulge] not by static troops in a Maginot Line, but by a vast mechanized U.S. Army fully mounted on wheels. In accepting the risk of enemy penetration into the Ardennes, we had counted heavily on the speed with which we could fling this mechanized strength against his flanks."[2]

Without trucks and drivers, the beleaguered U.S. troops who held the line in Belgium and Luxembourg would never have been supplied or even transported to the battlefield in time to stop the Germans.

Hundreds of trucks were also used to evacuate the huge stores of gasoline from the main POL reserve dumps located between Spa and Stavelot in Belgium and prevent them from falling into German hands. In one depot near Malmédy, Belgium, directly in the path of the German drive, trucks evacuated 1,115,000 gallons of MT80 (80-octane) gasoline and POL products. The operation was completed in forty-eight hours. A second depot, containing 2,226,000 gallons of gasoline, was evacuated in three and a half days from the evening of 18 December to the morning of 22 December.[3] One can speculate about the consequences to the Allies had these stocks been captured by the Germans.

Months before the Battle of the Bulge, Red Ball trucks had been hauling supplies to the sprawling depots at Liège, Charleroi, and Verdun or had transported materiel to railheads, where it was shipped to these depots by rail. The depots had been established to provide gasoline, ammunition, food, and clothing for the American drive into Germany. When the Wehrmacht struck on 16 December 1944, these supplies were available to use in stopping the German advance.

The old Red Ball provided an established organization and framework that enabled commanders to call for thousands of trucks to transport entire divisions into action within a matter of hours. The American Army had learned how to use trucks to maximum advantage in war, and much of this experience had been gained on the Red Ball.

Nowhere during World War II was this American mastery of mechanization and logistics more evident than in the Bulge. While many of his fellow commanders sniggered at his boastfulness, Patton, at Eisenhower's request, turned around a large portion of the Third Army in eastern France. He transported three divisions, largely by truck, north to the Ardennes, where they helped to stem the German advance and relieve the 101st Airborne Division at Bastogne, Belgium. Patton moved an entire corps—some sixty thousand men—more than 100 miles northwest, then northeast from the Saint-Avold area in France to the left flank of the Bulge that stretched from Echternach in Luxembourg to Bastogne. Without Patton's quick response, the Battle of the Bulge could have been an even more serious reversal for the Allies. In fact, Patton noted that, during the month-long Battle of the Bulge, trucks moved seventeen divisions an average distance of 100 miles to various points in Belgium and Luxembourg.

By December 1944, the ability of the Americans to shift divisions, corps, and even entire armies with the needed materiel was staggering. The First Army moved more than forty-eight thousand vehicles to the battle zone between 17 and 26 December, and the XII Corps redeployed thousands of men by truck to counter the German attack. Despite American concerns about the growing number of sidelined and overworked trucks, the U.S. Army somehow found enough of them during the Battle of the Bulge. According to Hugh Marshall Cole in *The Ardennes: Battle of the Bulge*: "There always was enough extra transport to meet unusual demands for supply and troop movement."[4]

The trucks helped to make the 101st Airborne Division's courageous stand at Bastogne legendary in American military annals. Just hours after the Germans attacked in the Bulge, vehicles from numerous trucking companies that had served on the Red Ball converged on Soissons, over the old Red Ball Highway in France, where the 101st was bivouacked and held in reserve for just such a crisis. The paratroopers were loaded into the cargo beds of Jimmies and onto semitrailers with some standing the entire trip, and driven through the night into Belgium and then on to Bastogne. As the first troopers began disembarking from the trucks, they went into action against the advancing Germans.

The operation to move the 101st to Bastogne began at dusk on 17 December. The first of some 3,801 trucks carrying the paratroopers arrived in Mourmelon, Belgium, about nine o'clock the next morning, and the last paratroopers arrived in combat by eight o'clock that evening.

The 82d Airborne division was also transported through the night by vehicles from various trucking units to the Werbomont area on the northern flank of the Bulge, where they arrived just in time to help stop Lt. Col. Jochen Peiper's tank columns. Peiper commanded Battlegroup Peiper, a spearhead unit of the Sixth SS Panzer Division, which pushed across the northern flank of the Bulge.

A log of the 146th QM Truck Company recalled the tensions of the hour:

> Reinforcements had to be found to stem the threatening tide of German success and it fell to the 82nd and 101st U.S. Airborne Divisions who were still licking their wounds after combat in support of the beleaguered British and Polish paratroops at Arnhem [the Netherlands], when Rudy Weber remembers the call to pick up airborne troops commanded by General [Anthony C.] McAuliffe and take them to Bastogne. . . .
>
> We drove all night, I don't know where we picked up these troops, I know we went through Sedan [France] and we were going toward Bastogne. . . .
>
> Rudy Weber dropped off his 82nd paratroopers . . . and right away they start digging foxholes right alongside the road. The guys I had on my truck, I dropped 'em off in the country and you could hear small arms fire. They said the Germans are just over the hill here. . . .
>
> Bill Albright brought up the 101st from Soissons. Bastogne was already encircled when we made the trip. I don't think those Airborne boys really enjoyed their trip because they were standing up. . . .
>
> Once the 146th had delivered their troops John Axselle remembers . . . the MPs had to wake the drivers up, they were dead beat from hauling these guys in and they'd pull up on the side of the road to get a little sleep and an MP come along and butted a carbine on the cab door. "You'd better get this shit wagon outa here. The Germans are coming," and they could hear the tanks, so they left![5]

James Chappelle described the fear that gripped the troops during the Battle of the Bulge. "The first time I really got scared was when I went to pick up troops of the 101st after the Germans made their breakthrough. Third platoon went out in COEs and then took the troops to the front. But those soldiers were more afraid than I was."[6]

The contrast between the logistics and transportation organizations of American and German armies was never more apparent than during the Battle of the Bulge. The Germans were defeated even before they began their attacks because they no longer had the ability to sustain a prolonged and costly advance. They were so low on gasoline reserves that their victory was predicated on the capture of vast American gasoline stocks, principally around Liège and Spa. Lack of gas led to transport deficiencies, which, in turn, led to ammunition shortages and more failures and deficiencies all the way down the line.[7]

Germany was also running out of trucks. New trucks coming off the production lines could not make up for those destroyed in the field during the Battle of the Bulge. Many of the Germans' trucks were worn out, foreign-made vehicles captured during earlier conquests. Many were simply abandoned by the roadside during the fighting.[8]

It is hard to believe that, even at that late date in a war of movement and mechanization, large portions of the German Army were still supplied by horse and wagon. "In fact, some of the German divisions in the Ardennes had more horses than German infantry divisions of 1918, and the supply lines over which they operated, in some cases, extended all the way back to the Rhine over bad roads that were subject constantly to allied air attacks. Many of the horses sickened and died."[9]

The Germans also experienced the same problems with horse-drawn supply trains in the Bulge as they had experienced in Russia in 1941. Horse-drawn supply or artillery columns mixed with the motorized traffic during the first days of the offensive and greatly slowed the distribution of supplies.[10]

Despite reeling from the German offensive in the Bulge, the Americans were in full control of their logistic situation during the entire battle. American troops seldom ran out of ammunition because, in part, they continued to use truckborne mobile supply dumps as they had on the Red Ball.[11]

The Germans never made it to Antwerp, their primary objective, to choke off supplies to the Allied armies, and materiel continued to pour into the continent during the battle. After the war, Army historians concluded that the German attack failed because the Wehrmacht high command and Hitler "understood neither the importance of supply nor its effective organization."[12] The Americans did understand such factors.

The role of motor transport in containing the Germans in the Bulge was highlighted by Maj. Gen. James M. Gavin in a letter to Brig. Gen. C. O. Thrasher, commanding general of the Oise Section of COMZ, who was responsible for dispatching the trucks to transport the airborne troops. The letter reads, in part:

> We have had a very interesting four weeks. The division succeeded in destroying a great part of the First SS Panzer Division, a small part of the Second SS Panzer Division and, I believe, the complete destruction of the 52nd Volks Grenadier Division. . . . All of this, however, was made possible by the promptness with which the transportation was made available to us to get up there and the unstinting and wholehearted cooperation in all your staff and subordinates, including your drivers.[13]

Once the Bulge was contained and the Germans thrown back, the stage was set for the final chapter of the ETO. In February 1945, the American armies began the final assault on Germany. As during the pursuit across France the previous summer, the Americans punched through negligible defenses to race to the Elbe. Once again, they outran the supply lines and forward depots. At times, armored forces were as much as 200 miles ahead of the closest supply depots.

The Red Ball had been retired, but the Army resurrected its ghost in the express trucking lines established to supply the fast-moving American forces in their drive across Germany. The lessons learned on the Red Ball Express were applied to the trucking lines in Germany in order to hasten the end of the war.

TWENTY-SIX

ABC TO XYZ

On 7 March 1945, Capt. Karl Timmerman, a company commander with the 9th Armored Division, advanced to a position near Remagen, Germany, to reconnoiter the Rhine River and the Ludendorff railroad bridge. Timmerman expected to see another devastated German town and the bridge to the east bank demolished by the usually thorough German Army engineers, and he was totally unprepared to find the bridge, intact and undamaged, still spanning the Rhine.

The Germans attempted to destroy the structure while Timmerman watched, but the demolition charges failed and the Americans moved on to capture the bridge. Within hours, thousands of U.S. troops were swarming over the span to establish a bridgehead on the east bank of the Rhine, the last obstacle protecting the Ruhr industrial area and the heart of Hitler's Germany. For months, the Allies had attempted to reach the Rhine, which no invading army had crossed since Napoleon's army in 1805. Field Marshal Montgomery had tried, and failed, to cross the Rhine during Operation Market Garden in September 1944. Troops of Bradley's First Army had attempted to push to the Rhine through the Aachen Gap from September to November 1944, with disastrous and failed attacks in Germany's Heurtgen Forest. Farther south, the Rhine had been Patton's objective since the breakout from Normandy in August 1944.

The success of the 9th Armored at Remagen was soon followed with additional Rhine crossings by Montgomery's 21st Army Group, Bradley's 12th Army Group, and Devers's 6th Army Group farther to the south. Germany lay exposed, and the Allies would soon reach the Elbe River to link up with Russian armies advancing from the east.

With the Rhine breached, five American armies, totaling some 1,617,000 men, began pouring over the river in a rapid advance against a disintegrating German Army that was a shadow of its former self. Old men and young boys, along with questionable recruits from occupied countries, held much of the German line against the oncoming armies. The battle for the German heartland soon resembled the pursuit of the German Army across France during August and September 1944. In many ways—the size of the Allied forces, the improvements in equipment, and the experience and professionalism of the soldiers—the pursuit across Germany surpassed the speed and excitement of the advance across France during the previous summer.

On 26 March 1945, Corporal Brice recorded the hectic events of those days during the battle for Germany:

> We are now engaged in a marathon run to keep reinforcements and supplies up with the fast moving armored columns and infantry as in the days after the breakout from St. Lô. Our drivers and trucks have taken an awful beating in the drive across France and we still have several of our original trucks that are all but falling to pieces. We must rise to the occasion however, since victory depends on our success in keeping troops and supplies up where they are needed. If a truck or a driver can move he or it is needed."[1]

The last seven weeks of the war in the ETO strained the logistics system to the limits. As was the case during the breakout from Normandy, the advancing combat units were far ahead of the supply depots. In February 1945, the gap between the front lines and the depots averaged about 50 miles. By May, it exceeded 250 miles.[2]

The bulk of the materiel being hauled to the front went in the cargo beds of trucks, and the distances traveled were becoming so great that it took longer and longer for supplies to reach their destinations. Often, the depots had moved on just as they had in France. William F. Ross and Charles F. Romanus, in *The Quartermaster Corps: Operations in the War against Germany*, noted:

> The increasing distances and congestion on the floating bridges across the Rhine caused the turnaround time of trucks moving between Trier and the advanced areas of the Third Army to reach thirty-six hours. Colonel [Everett] Busch of Third Army was hesitant about setting up a Class II and IV depot at Frankfurt. It would probably be too far to the rear before it began to operate.[3]

The First and Ninth Armies were experiencing the same problems. Their trucks had to travel distances often exceeding 400 miles to pick up and deliver supplies to the frontline troops. According to Ross and Romanus, "The monthly mileages reported were the highest in the history of continental operations."[4]

Although the advance into Germany was largely supplied by trucks, it would have been impossible without a Herculean effort by the Army's engineers. Robert Leckie notes:

> The American engineers showed a technological speed and skill that left their proud German counterparts filled with awe and envy. In a matter of days, 75,000 American engineers built sixty-two spans—forty-six pontoon, eleven fixed highway and five railway bridges—across the river. Using the Remagen bridgehead as a fulcrum, seven Allied armies went over the Rhine all along the north-uth line of the great river. They crossed in every conceivable way, Treadway and Bailey bridge, pontoons.[5]

Drivers had to use extreme caution in crossing many of these Rhine bridges, particularly in the larger, heavier tractor-trailers that were arriving in great numbers to replace the Jimmies.

Most of the bridging equipment used to span the Rhine was hauled to the river by truck. Welby Frantz, an officer in the 3923d QM Truck Company, transported ungainly sections of Bailey bridges from Aachen to Remagen. The trucks set out through an eerie blackout that enveloped them all the way to their destination. The trucks became lost, regrouped, and were stuck behind a tank recovery unit that was mired in the mud, but the bridging sections were finally delivered to the engineers outside Remagen. These sections were used to span the Rhine adjacent to the Remagen bridge, which had collapsed into the river after days of repeated air strikes by the Luftwaffe.[6]

The men of the 3630th QM Truck Company were also caught up in the excitement of the advance across Germany, which everyone knew would lead to victory in Europe. The unit historian reported:

> As March went by we could sense big things in the air. From the windows of St. Tround [France], we watched a constant stream of tanks, amphibious trucks, pontoons and Bailey Bridge equipment being rushed up to positions along the front lines in readiness for our big push across the Rhine. We were informed when, and if there was a big breakthrough, it would be our job to work in close support of units of the Ninth U.S. Army, hauling supplies directly to front line supply points, and that we would keep our trucks constantly on the move to assure the success of the operation."[7]

Many of the truck units transporting supplies to the front in Germany were organized into the XYZ Express, the last and largest of the long-haul motor truck lines in the ETO and also manned in the majority by blacks. The XYZ began operations on 25 March 1945, exactly seven months from the date that the Red Ball was inaugurated. The four XYZ routes extended eastward into Germany from four jumping-off points: Liège, Belgium; Düren, Germany; Luxembourg; and Nancy, France. The job of the XYZ drivers was to support four American armies, the Ninth, First, Third, and Seventh, as they advanced into the Reich.[8]

The XYZ was organized around 128 truck companies, many of them equipped with tractors and 10-ton trailers and 2,000-gallon gasoline carriers. At this stage in the war, the Jimmy was being phased out as the primary cargo carrier in the ETO. By V-E Day, 125 of the Motor Transport Service's 260 truck companies were equipped with either 4- to 5-ton truck-tractors or 10-ton semitrailers. Ninety-two truck companies had 2½-ton trucks, either the standard Jimmy or the COE type. The 10-ton semitrailers proved to be the most valuable vehicle for general-purpose cargo hauling, particularly over long distances, but the Army still loved the Jimmy.

The XYZ line averaged a daily lift of 12,859 tons during the last two months of the war. As during the pursuit across France, gasoline was the most important commodity. With hundreds of thousands more men and vehicles on the continent than in August 1944, the consumption of gasoline rose significantly. The depots at Liège and Verdun shipped 5,700,000 and 4,200,000 gallons, respectively, in January 1945. The same depots shipped 25,300,000 and 10,200,000 gallons, respectively, in March. The Army also maintained a reserve of 53,000,000 gallons of gasoline packed in jerricans for the northern armies of the 12th Army Group. The reserve of bulk gasoline totaled some 69,000,000 gallons stored in depots ranging from the Low Countries to the channel ports.[9]

Ross and Romanus noted that the XYZ Express "was the most orderly and efficient, as well as the largest, of the motor express operations. Notable improvements over Red Ball were in administration, traffic control, equipment, and coordination with other means of transportation, especially rail."[10] There was good reason for the improvements. Not only had the Army learned from the Red Ball, but four other express lines, besides XYZ, had been established since the days of the Red Ball. By March 1945, the Army was highly experienced in the operation of trucking lines.

The first of the express lines established after Red Ball was the White Ball Express, launched on 6 October 1944, to complement Red Ball operations. The White Ball's function was to transport materiel from the ports of Le Havre and Rouen to depots and rail transfer points around Paris, Beauvais, Compiègne, Soissons, and Reims. Most of the supplies were loaded at Rouen.

The White Ball operated until 10 January 1945, with as many as forty-eight truck companies working at one time. During the three months of White Ball's existence, its trucks carried some 140,486 tons of supplies, with an average daily haul of 1,614 tons. The average length of a White Ball trip was 113 miles.[11]

The Green Diamond Express was established on 14 October 1944 to move supplies from the Normandy depots to rail loading points at Avranches and Dol-de-Bretagne. The Green Diamond lasted only three weeks, until 1 November. The ever-present mud in Brittany and Normandy seriously affected its operations. When it ceased operations, the Green Diamond had carried an estimated 15,590 tons of supplies.[12]

The Red Lion Express was established to haul British gasoline and American supplies from Bayeux in Normandy to the 21st Army Group railhead in Brussels, Belgium, in support of the airborne operations in Holland during Operation Market Garden. The Red Lion operated for twenty-seven days, 16 September to 12 October 1944.

The U.S. Army provided the personnel for the Red Lion, and the British provided the camp and control sites, as well as many of the necessary supplies. At its conclusion, the line had carried some 17,556 tons of supplies, with an average daily haul of 650 tons. Eight U.S. truck companies were assigned to the Red Lion, with an average daily trip per truck of 306 miles.[13]

In December 1944, the Army created the Little Red Ball for express delivery of small quantities of supplies urgently needed at the front. Trains moving materiel from Cherbourg to Paris required three days to make the trip, whereas trucks could make deliveries in a single day.[14] The Little Red Ball route ran from Carentan to Paris over Highway N-13, and the trucks delivered 100 tons of materiel a day, mostly medical, signal, and chemical supplies. Little Red Ball operated with one truck company using 10-ton semitrailers and ran from 15 December 1944 to 17 January 1945.

The ABC (American-British-Canadian, but sometimes called Antwerp-Brussels-Charleroi) Express Line served the longest of any express line during the war. It was established to clear incoming supplies from the port of Antwerp. Trucks from fourteen companies took the supplies from the Antwerp surge pool or marshaling yard outside the port area and transported them over various routes to more forward Belgian depots at Liège, Mons, and Charleroi. The ABC line ran from 30 November 1944 to 26 March 1945, the day after the XYZ Express line was created.

During its 117 days of operation, the ABC carried nearly a quarter million tons of supplies over the 90 miles to depots and dumps that supplied the First and Ninth Armies during the final drives into Germany. The line's average daily haul was 2,092 tons.[15]

Although the ABC line was not the first to use tractors and 10-ton trailers, it perfected the use of these vehicles. The trucks hitched up to trailers in Antwerp and carried them to destinations where they were detached and shunted to unloading areas. A truck, also called a tractor, then picked up another trailer, often loaded with such items as spent shell casings, and transported it back to Antwerp. The historian of the 3630th QM Truck Company reported in the unit history:

> Day and night and through all kinds of weather our convoys rolled along the now numerous ABC Highways to Liège, Charleroi, Mons and Lille. Soon, we together with all the other ABC Companies were delivering an average of more than three

thousand tons of supplies daily from the Port of Antwerp, to forward dumps. This operation [ABC] started as an experiment and was probably the first time in the history of World War II that ten ton semi-tractors and trailers were used as a main source of hauling supplies to Front Line supply points.[16]

The use of tractors and trailers was applied with great success on the XYZ Express. During its sixty-three days of service from 25 March to 31 May, three weeks after the war was over, XYZ carried some 871,895 tons of supplies to U.S. troops advancing through Germany. To be sure, trucks of all varieties were used on the XYZ, but the preponderance of vehicles was the tractor and trailer.[17]

Another trucking operation was the 6957th Highway Transport Division (Provisional), which supported the Third Army on its march through Germany. The 6957th carried 354,015 tons of supplies forward. The average daily haul was 7,500 tons carried by some sixty-two truck companies, including thirty-four equipped with 10-ton semitrailers and fourteen with bulk tankers, each with a capacity of 2,000 gallons.[18]

The 6956th Highway Transport Division (Provisional), consisting of fifteen truck companies, operated during the later days of the war in support of the U.S. Ninth Army, the most northerly of the American field armies. Twelve of the fifteen companies were equipped with 10-ton semitrailers, and three companies operated with 2,000-gallon tanker trucks. By V-E Day, the 6956th's truckers had delivered 122,684 tons of supplies to forward depots.

The 6958th Highway Transport Division (Provisional) supported the U.S. First Army and reached a peak strength of thirty-one truck companies between 28 March and 8 May 1945. The division hauled a total of 182,425 tons of supplies.

Working with the U.S. Seventh Army was the 469th Quartermaster Group, which operated as a highway transport division over the Yellow Diamond route through southern Germany and Austria. Between 31 March 1945 and V-E Day, twenty trucking companies, seventeen of them using 10-ton semitrailers, operated over the Yellow Diamond and carried 146,000 tons of supplies to the advancing armies. The trucks on the Yellow Diamond were handicapped by the narrow roads that ran through mountainous terrain.

The Army had learned from the successes and failures of the Red Ball. During the final weeks of the war, it applied those lessons to the final drive. Discipline on the XYZ line was much improved over that of Red Ball. Trucks stayed in convoys and maintained constant speeds. MPs rode herd on errant vehicles, and traffic control points and regulating stations exercised greater control over the highways. Trucks were less likely to get lost, and, when they broke down, they were quickly repaired.

The use of 10-ton semitrailers also streamlined the transport of materiel. Loading times were reduced to accelerate the supply of the frontline units.

The use of air transports was also improved. The Army opened some twenty-five emergency airstrips east of the Rhine "for the delivery of unprecedented amounts of rations and gasoline to the forward areas of Twelfth Army Group."[19] Some of these airstrips were sections of German autobahn that could accommodate C-47 transport planes. As always, however, trucks were employed to carry supplies from the airplanes to the troops.

Pipelines for the delivery of gasoline were constructed under the Rhine, and decanting stations opened for trucks, which transported the gasoline into Germany.

The new American Army of 1945 was a juggernaut that was now as professional and experienced as any army on earth. Behind this powerful force was a penchant for mechanization and efficiency, exemplified by the Red Ball and other express trucking lines, that were the hallmarks of the American war machine and remain so to the present day. This military force was made possible by an industrial force, the likes of which the world had never before seen.

Eisenhower alluded to this awesome power in *Crusade in Europe*: "The combination of an overwhelming air force and the great mobility provided by the vehicular equipment of the Army enabled us to strike at any chosen point along a front of hundreds of miles."[20]

Patton expanded on this point: "America, as a nation, has the greatest ability for mass production of machines. It therefore behooves us to devise methods of war which exploit our inherent superiority. We must fight the war by machines on the ground, and in the air, to the maximum of our ability. . . ."[21]

TWENTY-SEVEN

THE RED BALL'S LEGACY

With the end of the war in the European Theater of Operations, the public quickly forgot the great logistics battles of 1944 and 1945. Even as the war wound to a close during the spring of 1945, the Red Ball was long gone and few Americans cared. They prayed only for victory and for an end to the killing. If they later had an interest in the war, they directed it to the glory of combat, not to the feats performed by transportation and logistics personnel.

Nevertheless, the Red Ball Express lived on in the minds of veterans of the ETO as one of the more enduring legends of World War II. The operation is remembered, in part, because it fits so well into American folklore. Americans have had a long love affair with the road and the truck. The speeding Red Ball drivers, thumbing their noses at military authority and the enemy to speed supplies to the front and to victory, symbolized American individualism and embodied the spirit of the frontiersmen and cowboys who had tamed the American continent. The Red Ball drivers were the first true road warriors, long before the truckers glorified in the song "Convoy" that rose to the top of the charts more than a quarter century later.

Numerous observers have made the connection between the Red Ball truckers and the American spirit that had been molded on the vast continent of North America. *Time* magazine, in September 1944, saw the Red Ball as symbolic of Americans "as a nation of builders and movers."[1] The military historian Chester Wilmot, in his classic work on World War II, *The Struggle for Europe,* noted that the Red Ball and the rapid American pursuit of the Germans across France represented "the survival, or revival, of the frontier spirit. The Americans had in their blood a longing for adventure and an instinct for movement, which they inherited from those pioneers who had broken out across the Alleghenies and opened up the Middle West."[2]

The Red Ball also lives on because it represents the one area of warfare—logistics—where the Americans excelled beyond all other armies. Critics, German and British alike, could denigrate the quality of American tanks, infantry, or tactics, but they stood in awe of the American Army's ability to move rapidly vast quantities of materiel and hundreds of thousands of men over great distances. They could not duplicate the American logistics effort. Certainly, the Germans were unprepared for the ability of the American Army to move such vast numbers of men and amounts of materiel against the Wehrmacht.

Wilmot, often highly critical of the American military, heaped praise on the American genius for movement and maneuver:

> The basic German miscalculation was the failure to appreciate that America's military prowess was a logical consequence of her industrial power. The Germans learned by experience that this power had given the American forces boundless equipment, but they did not realize that it had also provided a vast reservoir of manpower skilled in the use of machines.
>
> More than any other people, the Americans are mechanically minded. . . . In the realm of machines, the Americans possess a self-confidence, indeed a sense of mastery, which European people do not know. . . . To the American troops driving across France, distance meant nothing. They had no qualms about thrusting deep into the military unknown.[3]

Eisenhower, in *Crusade in Europe,* noted that the Soviets after the war "made one pressing demand on me. It was to explain the supply arrangements that enabled us to make the great sweep out of our constricted beachhead in Normandy to cover, in one rush, all of France, Belgium, and Luxembourg, up to the very borders of Germany."[4] During the summer and fall of 1944, the Red Ball Express was the star in this great logistical system.

The Red Ball also reflected the revolution that the truck brought to warfare, and its exploitation as a weapon by the American Army went far beyond that of the Wehrmacht during its blitzkriegs of 1940 and 1941. Historian Martin Van Creveld remarked that, in modern warfare, logistics comes close to being everything. He continued:

> Logistics make up as much as nine tenths of the business of war, and . . . the mathematical problems involved in calculating the movements and supply of armies are, to quote Napoleon, not unworthy of a Leibnitz or a Newton. As a great modern soldier (A. C. P. Wavell) has said: The more I see of war, the more I realize how it all depends on administration and transportation. . . . It takes little skill or imagination to see where you would like your army to be and when; it takes much knowledge and hard work to know where you can place your forces and whether you can maintain them there. A real knowledge of supply and movement factors must be the basis of every leader's plan; only then can he know how and when to take risks with those factors, and battles are won only by taking risks.[5]

Another reason the Red Ball is remembered and can never be forgotten is that the majority of the Red Ball troops were African American. They were asked to do the job of supplying Eisenhower's armies, and they performed it well.

The Red Ball earned such a revered place in the annals of America's wars that its name was resurrected during the Korean War and the Vietnam conflict. An express rail service in Japan that was used to rush critical supplies to Japanese ports for shipment to United Nations forces in Korea during the bleak summer of 1950 was nicknamed the Red Ball Express.[6] A trucking operation in Korea, to transport supplies from rear areas to the front, was also dubbed "The Red Ball Express."

The COMZ *Cadence,* a newspaper published in 1966 by the U.S. Army in France, published an article about a new Red Ball Express in Vietnam:

> Just as the Lone Ranger rides again—the Red Ball rolls again, only this time it's rolling in the Viet Nam War, delivering repair parts to front line troops within hours of receipt from the U.S. On this outing the "Red Ball Express" comes under the Army's First Logistical Command in the Republic of Viet Nam. . . . The Red Ball operation has immensely reduced . . . supply shortages in the "hot zones" and elsewhere in Viet Nam.[7]

The lessons and problems of the Red Ball were manifested forty-five years after World War II during the Gulf War and Operation Desert Storm. Although the nation's air and sealift capabilities were immensely greater in comparison to those of World War II, the troops in the field still had to be supplied and the military once again came up short of vehicles. A congressional report on the military aspects of the war noted that "throughout the operation . . . vehicle requirements far exceeded capabilities." As if referring to Red Ball, the report continued:

> The realization that available assets were being overwhelmed called for innovation by the small logistical staff. Heavy equipment transporters were requisitioned from the oil industry in Saudi Arabia as were buses to transport troops in the war zone. The magnitude of the transportation mission can be seen in statistics . . . on the movement of material by truck during the 21 days before the ground campaign began. More than 3,500 truck convoys—involving 1,400 Army and 2,100 Saudi vehicles— traveled more than 2,700 miles of MSR [main supply route]. These convoys logged more than 35 million miles. . . . [8]

The truck and the driver are still critical on the battlefield.

TRUCK
SPECIFICATIONS

Frank Buck

Standard Version of the 2½-Ton, Six-by-Six Cargo Truck, the Jimmy

Designed for all services, the standard version came with a 164-inch wheelbase. The cargo bay was equipped with troop seats for the transport of military personnel. The seats had "lazy" backs that folded to make way for cargo. A removable canvas top was supported by five bows and had roll-up straps to allow for ventilation. The cab had front and rear curtains with window flaps. Inside dimensions were 80 inches by 144 inches. The truck had a cargo capacity of 5,000 pounds and was available with or without a winch.

Physical Characteristics

Weight, without winch	15,450 lb.
Weight, with winch	16,450 lb.
Length, without winch	21 ft., 4 in.
Length, with winch	22 ft., 6 in.
Height, over bows	9 ft., 2 in.
Height, over cab	7 ft., 3³⁄₁₆ in.
Width	7 ft., 4 in.

Engine Specifications

Type	Valve-in-head
Number of cylinders	6
Bore	$3\frac{25}{32}$ in.
Stroke	4 in.
Displacement	269.52 cu. in.
Compression ratio	6.75 to 1
Horsepower	90

Robert Rubino

Short Wheelbase Version of the 2½-Ton, Six-by-Six Jimmy

This model, similar to the standard version of the 2½-ton truck, was built on a chassis with a 145-inch wheelbase. The body was also similar, but the inside dimensions were 80 inches by 108 inches. The vehicle had a payload of 5,350 pounds and came with or without a winch.

Physical Characteristics

Weight, without winch	15,350 lb.
Weight, with winch	16,450 lb.
Length, without winch	19 ft., 3 in.
Length, with winch	20 ft., 5 in.
Height, over bows	9 ft., 2 in.
Height, over cab	7 ft., 3¾₆ in.
Width	7 ft., 4 in.

Engine Specifications
(Same as Standard Version)

Type	Valve-in-head
Number of cylinders	6
Bore	3²⁵⁄₃₂ in.
Stroke	4 in.
Displacement	269.52 cu. in.
Compression ratio	6.75 to 1
Horsepower	90

Frank Buck

2½-Ton, Six-by-Six 15-Foot Cargo Truck— Cab over Engine

Like the standard Jimmy, the COE (cab over engine) model came with a 164-inch wheelbase but provided more cargo space because the engine was not situated in front of the cab. The drivers sat over the engine, and the cargo bed was extended in length. The truck had a payload of some 3,950 pounds and was designed to haul general cargo. The COE models did not come with a winch.

Physical Characteristics

Weight (gross)	14,760 lb.
Length	22 ft., 2¼ in.
Height, over bows	8 ft., 10 in.
Height, over cab	8 ft., 4 in.
Wheelbase	13 ft., 8 in.

Engine Specifications
(Same as Standard Version)

Type	Valve-in-head
Number of cylinders	6
Bore	3²⁵⁄₃₂ in.
Stroke	4 in.
Displacement	269.52 cu. in.
Compression ratio	6.75 to 1
Horsepower	90

Frank Buck

4- to 5-Ton, Four-by-Four Tractor Truck

The 4- to 5-ton, four-by-four tractor truck, with COE design, manufactured by Autocar, was used on the Red Ball and other express lines to tow 6-ton cargo semitrailers. The vehicle had single wheels at the front and dual wheels on the rear. Both sets of wheels could be powered. Power was supplied to all four wheels through a two-speed transfer case. A lever in the cab enabled the driver to declutch the front wheels when not required. The tractor came with either an open canvas-covered cab or a hard cab.

Physical Characteristics

Weight	21,010 lb.
Length	16 ft., 11½ in.
Width	7 ft., 11 in.
Height	9 ft., 4¼ in.
Wheelbase	11 ft., 2 in.

Engine Specifications

Type	In-line, liquid cool
Number of cylinders	6
Bore	4⅝ in.
Stroke	5¼ in.
Displacement	529 cu. in.
Compression ratio	110 at C.S.
Horsepower	112

2½-Ton, Six-by-Six Amphibian Truck (DUKW)

Along with the Jimmy, the DUKW (pronounced duck) was one of the great workhorses of World War II. Based on the standard 2½-ton, six-by-six truck, the DUKW had a watertight hull, with the truck chassis and drive units attached within the hull. For operations on land, the DUKW used all six driving wheels and conventional steering apparatus. In water, a propeller powered the vehicle, and it was steered by the front wheels and a rudder that interconnected with the steering column. The driver's compartment was open but had a removable top. The cargo compartment could hold up to twenty-five men or 5,000 pounds of cargo.

Physical Characteristics

Weight	19,570 lb.
Length ·	31 ft.
Width	8 ft., 2⅞ in.
Height, top up	8 ft., 9½ in.

Engine Specifications
(Same as Standard Version)

Type	Valve-in-head
Number of cylinders	6
Bore	$3^{25}/_{32}$ in.
Stroke	4 in.
Displacement	269.52 cu. in.
Compression ratio	6.75 to 1
Horsepower	90

Frank Buck

4- to 5-Ton, Four-by-Four Tractor Truck

The 4- to 5-ton, four-by-four tractor truck, COE design, manufactured by Federal, was used on the Red Ball and other express lines to tow 6 ton cargo semitrailers. The vehicle had single wheels at the front and dual wheels on the rear. Both sets of wheels could be powered. Power was supplied to all four wheels through a two-speed transfer case. A lever in the cab enabled the driver to declutch the front wheels when not required. The tractor was produced in two versions, an open, canvas-covered cab and a hard-covered cab. The Federal differed from the Autocar manufacture in very few ways. The sheet metal cover and transmission were somewhat different.

Physical characteristics and engine specifications are identical to those listed on p. 213.

■ INTRODUCTION

1. Welby Franz, interview with author, 1994.
2. Frank Buergler, interview with author, 1994.
3. Harold Rome, music and lyrics, "Red Ball Express," from *Call Me Mister*.
4. J. Eisenhower, *The Bitter Woods*, 77.

■ CHAPTER ONE: A FOOTHOLD IN NORMANDY

1. James Rookard, interview with author, July 1996.
2. Brice, *Journal of the 3909th Quartermaster Truck Company*, 20.
3. *Motor Transport Brigade*, 9–12.
4. Ibid., 11.
5. Ibid., 10.
6. Ibid., 9.
7. Headquarters, U.S. Army European Theater of Operations, Information and Education Division, Research Branch, *The Utilization of Negro Infantry Platoons in White Companies*, June 1945, 3.
8. John Houston, interview with author, August 1996.
9. James Rookard, interview with author, July 1996.
10. Washington Rector, interview with author, 1993.
11. James Blackwell and James Rookard, interviews with author, July 1996.
12. Brice, *Journal of the 3909th Quartermaster Truck Company*, 23.
13. Ibid.
14. Pyle, *Brave Men*, 259.
15. Ruppenthal, *Logistical Support*, 1:420.

16. Ibid., 1:432.

17. Butterton, *Metric 16*, 175.

18. Giles, G.I. *Journal of Sergeant Giles*, 76.

■ Chapter Two: Operation Cobra

1. Pogue, *Supreme Command*, 192. These figures include 73,000 U.S. casualties and 49,000 suffered by British and Canadian forces.

2. Leckie, *Delivered from Evil*, 737.

3. Pyle, *Brave Men*, 298.

4. Quoted in Keegan, *Second World War*, 394.

5. Pyle, *Brave Men*, 298.

6. D'Este, *Decision in Normandy*, 401.

7. Bradley and Blair, *A General's Life*, 210.

8. Quoted in Mayo, *Ordnance Department on Beachhead and Battlefront*, 269.

■ Chapter Three: Breakout and Pursuit

1. Eisenhower, *Crusade in Europe*, 337.

2. Keegan, *Second World War*, 403.

3. Ibid., 410.

4. Fuller, *Second World War*, 327.

5. Eisenhower, *Crusade in Europe*, 291.

6. Ruppenthal, *Logistical Support*, 2:4–7.

7. Eisenhower, *Crusade in Europe*, 291.

8. Ruppenthal, *Logistical Support*, 2:6.

9. Ibid.

10. Ibid.

11. Mayo, *Ordnance Department on Beachhead and Battlefront*, 262.

12. Brice, *Journal of the 3909th Quartermaster Truck Company*, 25.

13. Ibid., 26.

14. Blumenson, *Breakout and Pursuit*, 688–9.

15. Brice, *Journal of the 3909th Quartermaster Truck Company*, 45.

16. Ibid., 26.

■ Chapter Four: In Harm's Way

1. Mayo, *Ordnance Department on Beachhead and Battlefront*, 275.

2. William Harnist, interview with author, 1997.

3. *476th QM Group, Unit History*, 3.

4. Mayo, *Ordnance Department on Beachhead and Battlefront*, 274.

5. Blumenson, *Breakout and Pursuit*, 669.

6. Davis, *Patton's Wheels*, 3.

7. *Motor Transport Brigade*, 9.

8. Quoted in Brice, *Journal of the 3909th Quartermaster Truck Company*, 30.

9. Quoted in Lee, *Employment of Negro Troops*, 640.

10. Brice, *Journal of the 3909th Quartermaster Truck Company*, 26.

11. *Motor Transport Brigade*, 9.

12. Mayo, *Ordnance Department on Beachhead and Battlefront*, 263.

13. Quoted in Nichols, *Ernie's War*, 293.

14. Brice, *Journal of the 3909th Quartermaster Truck Company*, 32–33.

15. Ibid., 47.

16. Ibid., 34.

■ Chapter Five: The Ports

1. Ruppenthal, *Logistical Support*, 1:464.

2. Ibid.

3. Ibid., 1:187.

4. Ibid.

5. Ross and Romanus, *Quartermaster Corps*, 406.

6. Blumenson, *Breakout and Pursuit*, 415.

7. Ibid., 340.

8. Keegan, *Second World War*, 411.

9. Ruppenthal, *Logistical Support*, 1:465.

10. Ibid., 2:96.

11. Fuller, *Second World War*, 332.

12. Ibid., 333.

13. Ruppenthal, *Logistical Support*, 2:49.

▪ CHAPTER SIX: THE RED BALL GETS ROLLING

1. Bradley and Blair, *A General's Life*, 285.

2. Eisenhower, *Crusade in Europe*, 290.

3. Ibid.

4. Van Creveld, *Supplying War*, 146.

5. Harrison, *Cross Channel Attack*, 223.

6. Ibid., 224.

7. Ibid., 230.

8. *Motor Transport Brigade*, 14.

9. Huston, *Sinews of War*, 529.

10. Ruppenthal, *Logistical Support*, 1:309.

11. *Motor Transport Brigade*, 3.

12. John O'Leary, interview with author, 1995.

13. Earl Swallow, letter to author, 1995.

14. Roy Benner, letter to author, 1995.

15. James Rookard, interview with author, 1997.

16. Ross and Romanus, *Quartermaster Corps*, 414–5.

17. Quoted in Bass, *Precious Cargo*, 130.

18. Earl Swallow, letter to author, 1995.

19. Phillip Dick, interview with author, 1995.

20. Diemer, *This Is It*, 18.

21. Ibid., 3.

22. Davis, *Patton's Wheels*, 3.

23. Ibid.

24. Bass, *Precious Cargo*, 128.

25. Quoted in ibid., 129.

26. Ibid., 130.

■ CHAPTER SEVEN: THE BLOOD OF WAR

1. Bradley and Blair, *A General's Life*, 321.

2. Ruppenthal, *Logistical Support*, 1:504–5.

3. Ibid., 1:505.

4. Washington Rector, interview with author, 1994.

5. *The Stars and Stripes*, 31 August 1944.

6. John Shevlin, interview with author, 1995.

7. Farago, *Patton, Ordeal and Triumph*, 585.

8. Charles Stevenson, interview with author, 1995.

9. Ruppenthal, *Logistical Support*, 1:505.

10. Charles Stevenson, interview with author, 1995.

11. Farago, *Patton, Ordeal and Triumph*, 592.

12. Ruppenthal, *Logistical Support*, 1:506.

13. Blumenson, *The Patton Papers*, 531.

14. Farago, *Patton, Ordeal and Triumph*, 588.

15. Blumenson, *Breakout and Pursuit*, 601.

16. Ibid.

17. Pyle, *Brave Men*, 317.

18. Ruppenthal, *Logistical Support*, 1:578.

19. Ibid., 2:31.

20. Ibid., 1:511.

■ CHAPTER EIGHT: OVER THE BEACHES, INTO THE MUD

1. Beck, *The Corps of Engineers*, 344.

2. Bass, *Precious Cargo*, 120.

3. Huston, *Sinews of War*, 493.

4. G-4 Histories, *Red Ball*, 8.

5. Ibid.

6. Bass, *Precious Cargo*, 128.

7. Charles Stevenson, interview with author, 1995.

■ CHAPTER NINE: STRANGERS IN WHITE AMERICA

1. Quoted by Robert Emerick, interview with author, 1995.

2. James Rookard, interview with author, 1996.

3. J. H. Sherman, *New Republic*, 19 November 1945, 677–8.

4. Lee, *Employment of Negro Troops*, 23.

5. James Rookard, interview with author, 1996.

6. Anonymous officer who commanded black troops, interview with author, 1995.

7. Moore, *To Serve My Country*, 31.

8. Lee, *Employment of Negro Troops*, 15–20.

9. Ibid., 704.

10. Ibid., 592–3.

11. Ibid., 593.

12. Ibid., 231, 238.

■ CHAPTER TEN: THE ODYSSEY OF THE 514TH

1. James Rookard, interview with author, July 1996.

2. James Chappelle, interview with author, July 1996.

3. Jack Blackwell, interview with author, July 1996.

4. Lee, *Employment of Negro Troops*, 366.

5. Ibid., 372.

6. James Chappelle, interview with author, July 1996.

7. James Rookard, interview with author, July 1996.

8. Herman Heard, interview with author, July 1996.

9. Brice, *Journal of the 3909th Quartermaster Truck Company*, 12.

10. Ibid., 13.

11. Longmate, *The G.I.s*, 124–5.

12. Brice, *Journal of the 3909th Quartermaster Truck Company*, 16.

13. Ibid.
14. Charles Stevenson, interview with author, 1995.
15. James Rookard, interview with author, July 1996.
16. Quoted in Reynolds, *Rich Relations*, 218.
17. James Rookard, interview with author, July 1996.
18. Charles Stevenson, interview with author, 1995.
19. Ibid.
20. William Harnist, interview with author, 1996.
21. James Chappelle, interview with author, 1996.
22. Brice, *Journal of the 3909th Quartermaster Truck Company*, 19.

▪ CHAPTER ELEVEN: EFFECTIVE CHAOS

1. G-4 Histories, *Red Ball*, 13.
2. *Company K*, Unit History, 6.
3. G-4 Histories, *Red Ball*, 13.
4. Ibid., 14.
5. Ibid., 13.
6. Ibid., 24–5.
7. Ibid., 24.
8. Ibid., 25.
9. Ibid., 56.
10. Ibid., 31.
11. Tyrrell, *History of the 804th Military Police Company*, 17.
12. Quoted in Hines, *History of the General Purpose Vehicle*, 150.
13. Ibid., 150–1.
14. G-4 Histories, *Red Ball*, 37.
15. Ibid.
16. Ibid., 69.
17. Ibid., 3.
18. Ibid.
19. Ibid., 13.

■ **Chapter Twelve: Across the Seine**

1. Allen, *Drive to Victory*, 89.
2. Bradley and Blair, *A General's Life*, 321.
3. Ibid., 321–2.
4. Ibid., 322.
5. Giles, *G.I. Journal of Sergeant Giles*, 87.
6. Bass, *Precious Cargo*, 135.
7. Brice, *Journal of the 3909th Quartermaster Truck Company*, 37–8.
8. Matisoff, *History of the 62nd QM Base Depot*, 7.
9. Weigley, *Eisenhower's Lieutenants*, 281.
10. Ruppenthal, *Logistical Support*, 1:570.

■ **Chapter Thirteen: Never Volunteer**

1. Philo Rockwell King III, letter to author, 1995.
2. Phillip Dick, interview with author, 1994.
3. Ibid.
4. Ibid.
5. Merle Gutherie, interview with author, 1994.
6. Phillip Dick, interview with author, 1994.
7. Ibid.
8. John Rearigh, interview with author, 1995.
9. Resley Hibshman and Fred Schlunz, letters to author, 1994.
10. Kenneth Duncan, interview with author, 1994.
11. Anonymous, interview with author, 1994.
12. Ibid.

■ **Chapter Fourteen: Red Ball Trucks Don't Brake**

1. William Coursey, interview with author, 1994.
2. Fred Reese, interview with author, 1994.
3. James Rookard, interview with author, July 1996.
4. Herman Heard, interview with author, July 1996.
5. Quoted in G-4 Histories, *Red Ball*, 41.

6. Paul Anderson, interview with author, 1994.

7. G-4 Histories, *Red Ball*, 63.

8. Quoted in Motley, *Invisible Soldier*, 189.

9. G-4 Histories, *Red Ball*, 64.

10. Robert Emerick, interview with author, 1994.

11. Ibid.

12. Fred Reese, interview with author, 1994.

13. Quoted in G-4 Histories, *Red Ball*, 38.

14. Booker Nance, interview with author, 1994, 1996.

15. Herman Heard, interview with author, 1996.

16. Robert Emerick, interview with author, 1994.

17. John Houston, interview with author, 1996.

18. James Rookard, interview with author, 1997.

19. Kenneth Duncan, interview with author, 1994.

20. Charles Barber, interview with author, 1994.

21. Robert Emerick, interview with author, 1994.

22. Ibid.

■ **CHAPTER FIFTEEN: DAILY LIFE ON THE RED BALL**

1. Niedler, *History of the 894th Ordnance H.A.M. Co.*, Unit History, 24.

2. Ibid.

3. Charles Stevenson, interview with author, 1994.

4. Company K, Unit History, 8.

5. Brice, *Journal of the 3909th Quartermaster Truck Company*, 36.

6. Brice, *Journal of the 3909th Quartermaster Truck Company*, 40–41.

7. Bass, *Precious Cargo*, 129.

8. Brice, *Journal of the 3909th Quartermaster Truck Company*, 35, 38.

9. G-4 Histories, *Red Ball*, 5.

10. Bass, *Precious Cargo*, 126.

11. Niedler, *History of the 894th Ordnance H.A.M. Co.*, Unit History, 24.

12. Diemer, *This Is It*, 19.

13. Hines, *History of the General Purpose Vehicle*, 147.

14. Brice, *Journal of the 3909th Quartermaster Truck Company*, 36.

15. James Chappelle, interview with author, July 1996.

16. Philo Rockwell King III, letter to author, 1994.

17. Anonymous, interview with author, 1997.

■ Chapter Sixteen: Temptations and Black Markets

1. Robert Emerick, interview with author, 1994.

2. James Rookard, interview with author, 1997.

3. Charles Stevenson, interview with author, 1994.

4. William Harnist, interview with author, 1997.

5. Anonymous, interview with author, 1997.

6. Ibid.

7. Philo Rockwell King III, letter to author, 1994.

8. Charles Stevenson, interview with author, 1994.

9. James Bailey, interview with author, 1996.

10. Anonymous, interview with author, 1997.

11. Robert Emerick, interview with author, 1994.

12. Anonymous, interview with author, 1997.

13. Ibid.

14. G-4 Histories, *Red Ball*, 41.

15. Quoted in Bass, *Precious Cargo*, 130.

16. Merle Gutherie, interview with author, 1995.

17. William Harnist, interview with author, 1996.

18. *Stars and Stripes*, quoted in G-4 Histories, *Red Ball*, 40.

19. *Newsweek*, 8 January 1945.

20. *Life* Magazine, 26 March 1945.

21. *Yank*, 4 May 1945.

22. Bass, *Precious Cargo*, 141.

23. *Yank*, 4 May 1945.

24. Anonymous, interview with author, 1997.

■ Chapter Seventeen: Secret Weapon

1. Risch and Kieffer, *The Quartermaster Corps: Organization, Supply and Services*, 2:322.
2. Van Creveld, *Supplying War*, 144.
3. Ibid., 145.
4. Ibid., 144.
5. Thompson and Mayo, *Ordnance Department*, 265.
6. Ibid., 296.
7. Quoted in Reynolds, *Rich Relations*, 368–9.
8. Data from Mayo, *Ordnance Department on Beachhead and Battlefront*, 296.
9. Bradley and Blair, *A General's Life*, 41.
10. *The Palimpsest*, Iowa State Historical Department, May/June 1975, 66.
11. Bradley and Blair, *A General's Life*, 54.
12. Van Creveld, *Supplying War*, 144.
13. *Time*, 25 September 1944.
14. Ibid.
15. Quoted in Col. Bruce H. Williams. Conversations between Gen. James A. Van Fleet and Col. Williams. Senior Army Debriefing Program. U.S. Army Military History Institute, Carlisle Barracks, Pa., 3 March 1973.

■ Chapter Eighteen: The Jimmy

1. Thompson and Mayo, *Ordnance Department*, 275.
2. Robert Rubino, interview with author, 1997.
3. Gunther Ctortnik, interview with author, 1997.
4. Van Creveld, *Fighting Power*, 192.
5. Lee Holland, interview with author, 1996.
6. Niedler, *History of the 894th Ordnance H.A.M. Co.*, 24.
7. Lee Holland, interview with author, 1996.

8. Robert Rubino, interview with author, 1999.

9. Thompson and Mayo, *Ordnance Department*, 266.

10. Ibid., 267.

11. Ibid., 268–9.

12. Ibid., 271.

13. Ibid., 275.

14. Manuel Rogers, interview with author, 1998.

■ CHAPTER NINETEEN: THE UBIQUITOUS JERRICAN

1. Charles Stevenson, interview with author, 1994.

2. Ruppenthal, *Logistical Support*, 2:202.

3. Ibid., 2:203–5.

4. Frank Buergler, interview with author, 1994.

5. Ruppenthal, *Logistical Support*, 2:201.

■ CHAPTER TWENTY: EXHAUSTED JIMMIES

1. Ruppenthal, *Logistical Support*, 2:243.

2. Thompson and Mayo, *Ordnance Department*, 298.

3. Brice, *Journal of the 3909th Quartermaster Truck Company*, 39.

4. Charles Stevenson, interview with author, 1994.

5. United States Army, European Theater of Operations, Communications Zone, Historical Section, G-4 Com Z, *History of G-4 Com Z*, 14.

6. G-4 Histories, *Red Ball*, 55.

7. Ibid., 38.

8. Ibid., 39.

9. Thompson and Mayo, *Ordnance Department*, 451.

10. Ibid., 454.

11. G-4 Histories, *Red Ball*, 59.

12. Ibid., 59, 60.

13. Quoted in Thompson and Mayo, *Ordnance Department*, 315.

14. Ibid., 283.

15. Ibid., 300.
16. Quoted in ibid.
17. Ibid., 301.
18. G-4 Histories, *Red Ball*, 65.
19. Ibid.
20. Robert Emerick, interview with author, 1994.
21. G-4 Histories, *Red Ball*, 65.
22. Ruppenthal, *Logistical Support*, 2:244.
23. Charles Stevenson, interview with author, 1994.
24. Thompson and Mayo, *Ordnance Department*, 300.
25. Ibid.
26. Ibid., 269.

■ CHAPTER TWENTY-ONE: TRAINS AND PLANES

1. G-4 Histories, *Red Ball*, 43.
2. Matisoff, *History of the 62nd QM Base Depot*, 11.
3. Army Corps of Engineers, *History of the 341st Engineers, July 29, 1943–March, 1946*, 8.
4. Ruppenthal, *Logistical Support*, 1:578.
5. Ibid., 1:572–83.
6. Ibid.

■ CHAPTER TWENTY-TWO: BUZZ BOMB ALLEY

1. *Company K*, Unit History, 9.
2. 3611 Quartermaster Truck Company. *Historical Summary*. Reunion, 19–29 September, 1986, 2.
3. Quoted in ibid.
4. James Chappelle, interview with author, 1996.
5. Merle Gutherie, interview with author, 1995.
6. High Hedge History, 25 June 1943–8 May 1945. Unit History, *283 Field Artillery Battalion*, 18.
7. Charles Weko, interview with author, 1994.

8. Davis, *Patton's Wheels*, 15.
9. Farago, *Patton, Ordeal and Triumph*, 643.
10. Bass, *Precious Cargo*, 129.
11. Brice, *Journal of the 3909th Quartermaster Truck Company*, 36.

■ CHAPTER TWENTY-THREE: JOINING THE INFANTRY

1. Weigley, *Eisenhower's Lieutenants*, 727.
2. Ibid.
3. Quoted in Motley, *Invisible Soldier*, 190.
4. James Chappelle, interview with author, 1996.
5. James Rookard, interview with author, 1996.
6. Quoted in J. H. Sherman, *New Republic*, 19 November 1945.
7. Lee, *Employment of Negro Troops*, 693.
8. Ibid., 695.
9. Quoted in ibid., 702.
10. Quoted in Motley, *Invisible Soldier*, 189.
11. Quoted in ibid., 159.
12. Quoted in ibid.
13. *Stars and Stripes*, 15 September 1944.
14. Motley, *Invisible Soldier*, 188.
15. James Rookard, interview with author, 1996.
16. Motley, *Invisible Soldier*, 192.
17. Charles Weko, interview with author, 1994.
18. Quoted in Motley, *Invisible Soldier*, 192.
19. James Rookard, interview with author, 1996.

■ CHAPTER TWENTY-FOUR: THE FINAL DAYS

1. Transportation School, *Express Line of Communication Motor Hauls*, 4–8.
2. Ibid.
3. G-4 Histories, *Red Ball*, 68.

4. Ibid., 69.
5. Ibid.
6. Ibid., 70.
7. Quoted in Bass, *Precious Cargo*, 135.

■ CHAPTER TWENTY-FIVE: VICTORY IN THE BULGE

1. Leckie, *Delivered from Evil*, 825.
2. Bradley, *A Soldier's Story*, 454–5.
3. Marshall, *The Ardennes*, 667.
4. Ibid., 666.
5. Bass, *Precious Cargo*, 142–3.
6. James Chappelle, interview with author, 1996.
7. Marshall, *The Ardennes*, 666–7.
8. Ibid.
9. Ibid.
10. Ibid.
11. Ibid., 665–7.
12. 3603 QM Truck Co. (HV) (TC), *Unit Operational Summary*, 7.
13. Ibid.

■ CHAPTER TWENTY-SIX: ABC TO XYZ

1. Brice, *Journal of the 3909th Quartermaster Truck Company*, 67.
2. Ross and Romanus, *Quartermaster Corps*, 434.
3. Ibid.
4. Ibid.
5. Leckie, *Delivered from Evil*, 897.
6. Welby Franz, interview with author, 1994.
7. 3603 QM Truck Co. (HV) (TC), *Unit Operational Summary*, 11.
8. Ross and Romanus, *Quartermaster Corps*, 435.
9. Ibid., 674.
10. Ibid., 339.

11. Bykofsky and Larson, *Transportation Corps*, 335.

12. Ibid.

13. Ibid.

14. Ruppenthal, *Logistical Support*, 2:143.

15. Bykofsky and Larson, *Transportation Corps*, 336.

16. *Company K*, Unit History, 11.

17. Ibid.

18. Bykofsky and Larson, *Transportation Corps*, 337.

19. Ross and Romanus, *Quartermaster Corps*, 434.

20. Eisenhower, *Crusade in Europe*, 453.

21. Patton, *War as I Knew It*, 366.

■ Chapter Twenty-Seven: The Red Ball's Legacy

1. *Time*, 25 September 1944.

2. Wilmot, Struggle for Europe, 427.

3. Ibid.

4. Eisenhower, *Crusade in Europe*, 309.

5. Van Creveld, *Supplying War*, 231–7.

6. Appleman, *South to Naktong, North to Yalu*, 260.

7. OMZ *Cadence*, 18 May 1966.

8. *Conduct of the Persian Gulf War*, Final Report to Congress, April 1992, Appendices A–S, p-F-45.

Books

Allen, Col. Robert S. *Drive to Victory*. New York: Berkley Publishing, 1947.

Ambrose, Stephen E. *D-Day, June 6, 1944, The Climactic Battle of World War II*. New York: Simon & Schuster, 1994.

Appleman, Roy. *South to the Naktong, North to the Yalu, June–November, 1950*. Washington, D.C.: Office of the Chief of Military History, Department of the Army, 1961.

Bass, Richard T. *Precious Cargo, The History of the U.S. Army 146th QM Truck Co.* Exeter-Devon, United Kingdom: Lee Publishing, 1993.

Beck, Alfred M. *The Corps of Engineers: The War against Germany*. Washington, D.C.: Office of the Chief of Military History, Department of the Army, 1985.

Blumenson, Martin. *Breakout and Pursuit*. Washington, D.C.: Office of the Chief of Military History, Department of the Army, 1961.

———. *The Patton Papers, 1940–1945*. Boston: Houghton Mifflin, 1974.

Bradley, Omar. *A Soldier's Story*. New York: Henry Holt and Company, 1951.

Bradley, Omar, and Clay Blair. *A General's Life*. New York: Simon & Schuster, 1983.

Buchanan, Russell A. *Black Americans in World War II*. Santa Barbara, Calif.: Clio Books, 1977.

Bykofsky, Joseph, and Harold Larson. *The Transportation Corps: Operations Overseas*. Washington, D.C.: Office of the Chief of Military History, Department of the Army, 1957.

Cole, Hugh Marshall. *The Lorraine Campaign*. Washington, D.C.: Office of the Chief of Military History, Department of the Army, 1950.

———. *The Ardennes: Battle of the Bulge*. Washington, D.C.: Office of the Chief of Military History, Department of the Army, 1983.

D'Este, Carlo. *Decision in Normandy*. New York: E. P. Dutton, 1983.

———. *Patton, a Genius for War*. New York: Harper Collins, 1995.

Eisenhower, Dwight D. *Crusade in Europe*. Garden City, N.Y.: Doubleday & Company, 1948.

Eisenhower, John D. *The Bitter Woods*. New York: Putnam, 1969.

Esposito, Vincent J. *The West Point Atlas of American Wars*. New York: Frederick A. Praeger, 1964.

Farago, Ladislas. *Patton, Ordeal and Triumph*. New York: Ivan Obolensky, Inc., 1963.

Freidin, Seymour, and William Richardson, eds. *The Fatal Decisions*. New York: Berkley Publishing, 1958.

Fuller, J. F. C. *The Second World War*. New York: Duell, Sloan and Pearce, 1962.

Giles, Janice Holt. *The G.I. Journal of Sergeant Giles*. Boston: Houghton Mifflin, 1965.

Harrison, Gordon. *Cross Channel Attack*. Washington, D.C.: Office of the Chief of Military History, Department of the Army, 1951.

Hart, B. H. Liddell. *History of the Second World War*. New York: G. P. Putnam's Sons, 1970.

Huston, James A. *The Sinews of War, Army Logistics, 1775–1953*. Washington, D.C.: Office of the Chief of Military History, Department of the Army, 1966.

Keegan, John. *The Second World War*. New York: Penguin Books, 1989.

Leckie, Robert. *Delivered from Evil*. New York: Harper & Row, 1987.

Lee, Ulysses. *The Employment of Negro Troops*. Washington, D.C.: Office of the Chief of Military History, Department of the Army, 1966.

Longmate, Norman. *The G.I.s, the Americans in Britain, 1942–1945*. New York: Charles Scribner's Sons, 1975.

MacGregor, Morris J., Jr. *Integration of the Armed Forces, 1940–1965*. Washington, D.C.: Center of Military History, United States Army, 1981.

Mayo, Lida. *The Ordnance Department on Beachhead and Battlefront*.

Washington, D.C.: Office of the Chief of Military History, Department of the Army, 1968.

Moore, Brenda L. *To Serve My Country, to Serve My Race*. New York: New York University Press, 1996.

Motley, Mary Penick. *The Invisible Soldier, the Experience of the Black Soldier in World War II*. Detroit: Wayne State University Press, 1975.

Nichols, David. *Ernie's War, the Best of Ernie Pyle's World War II Dispatches*. New York: Simon & Schuster, 1986.

Patton, George S. *War as I Knew It*. Boston: Houghton Mifflin Co., 1947.

Pogue, Forrest C. *The Supreme Command*. Washington: Office of the Chief of Military History, Department of the Army, 1954.

Pyle, Ernie. *Brave Men*. New York: Gosset & Dunlap, 1945.

Reynolds, David. *Rich Relations, The American Occupation of Britain 1942–1945*. London: Harper Collins, 1995.

Risch, Erna, and Chester Kieffer. *The Quartermaster Corps: Organization, Supply and Services*. Vols. 1 and 2. Office of the Chief of Military History, Department of the Army, 1953–55.

Ross, William F., and Charles F. Romanus. *The Quartermaster Corps: Operations in the War against Germany*. Washington, D.C.: Office of the Chief of Military History, Department of the Army, 1965.

Ruppenthal, Roland. *Logistical Support of the Armies*, vol. 1. Washington, D.C.: Office of the Chief of Military History, Department of the Army, 1953.

Ruppenthal, Roland. *Logistical Support of the Armies*, vol. 2. Washington, D.C.: Office of the Chief of Military History, Department of the Army, 1959.

Thompson, Harry C., and Lida Mayo. *The Ordnance Department: Procurement and Supply*. Washington, D.C.: Office of the Chief of Military History, Department of the Army, 1960.

Van Creveld, Martin. *Fighting Power: German Military Performance, 1914–1945*. Washington, D.C.: Office of Net Assessment, Department of Defense, 1980.

———. *Supplying War, Logistics from Wallenstein to Patton*. Cambridge: Cambridge University Press, 1977.

Wardlow, Chester. *The Transportation Corps: Movements, Training and*

Supply. Washington, D.C.: Office of the Chief of Military History, Department of the Army, 1956.

————. *The Transportation Corps: Responsibilities, Organization, and Operations*. Washington, D.C.: Office of the Chief of Military History, Department of the Army, 1951.

Weigley, Russell F. *Eisenhower's Lieutenants*. Bloomington: Indiana University Press, 1981.

Wilmot, Chester. *The Struggle for Europe*. Harper & Brothers, 1952.

Unit Histories

Battery A, 379th Field Artillery Battalion. *History of Battery A 379th F.A. BN., 102nd Division, September 15, 1942 to September 15, 1945*.

Brice, Cpl. Edwin L. *Journal of the 3909th Quartermaster Truck Company*. 1945.

Butterton, Meredith L. *Metric 16, History of the 126th Ordnance Company*. Durham, N.C.: Moore Publishing Co., 1972.

Company K, 467th QM Truck Regiment, Redesignated 3630 QM Truck Company, Unit History, n.d.

Davis, T/Sgt. Sarah M. *Patton's Wheels, The Story of Quartermaster Trucks in Third Army*. 1945.

Diemer, Eugene V. *This Is It: History of the 513th QM Group (TC)* [Transportation Corps]. U.S. Army, 1943–1945.

Duggan, Thomas V. *History of the 234th Engineer Combat Battalion*. T. V. Duggan, Maywood, N.J., 1947.

G-4 Histories, *Red Ball*. European Theater of Operations, Historical Division, Administrative File, 3 February 1942–1946.

Hines, William M. *History of the General Purpose Vehicle 1941–45: Its Availability in the European Theater of Operations, Maintenance Bulletin No. 11*. Headquarters, USFET, U.S. Army, 1945/46.

Matisoff, Col. Maurice. *History of the 62nd QM Base Depot*. Headquarters, 62nd QM Base Depot. 1944–45.

Motor Transport Brigade, Unit History, National Archives, n.d.

Niedler, Fred J. *History of the 894th Ordnance H.A.M. Co*. 1945.

Standing Operating Procedure, No. 8, Red Ball Express. Headquarters, European Theater of Operations, United States Army. 12 May 1944.

Standing Operating Procedure, No. 53, Red Ball Motor Transport Opera-

tions. Headquarters, European Theater of Operations, United States Army. For Col. Ross B. Warren. 2 December 1944.

476th QM Group, Unit History. n.d.

3603 QM Truck Co. (HV) [Heavy Vehicles] (TC) [Transportation Corps]. *Unit Operational Summary*. 29 June 1945.

3611 Quartermaster Truck Company, *Historical Summary*. Reunion, 19–20 September 1986.

3623 QM Truck Co. (TC) [Transportation Corps]. *High Hedge History, Unit History*. n.d.

283rd Field Artillery Battalion, Unit History, 25 June 1943 to 8 May 1945. 1945.

Transportation School, *Express Line of Communication Motor Hauls (Historical Record & Operational Study)*. Highway Unit Training Pamphlet No. 7, Fort Eustis, Va, 1949.

Tyrrell, Francis J. *History of the 804th Military Police Company*. 1945.

United States Army, European Theater of Operations, Communications Zone, Historical Section, G-4, Com Z. *History of G-4 Com Z, European Theater of Operations, Section III, Supply by Road, Air, and Water*. Washington, D.C.: Office of the Chief of Military History, Department of the Army, 1946.

United States Army, European Theater of Operations, Information and Education Division, Research Branch. *The Utilization of Negro Infantry Platoons in White Companies*. Washington, D.C.: Office of the Chief of Military History, Department of the Army, June 1949.

United States Army Corps of Engineers. *History of the 341st Engineer Regiment, July 29, 1943–March, 1946*. 1946.

Oral Histories

Williams, Col. Bruce H. Conversations between Gen. James A. Van Fleet and Col. Williams. Senior Army Debriefing Program. U.S. Army Military History Institute, Carlisle Barracks, Pa. 3 March 1973.

Interviews

Paul Anderson, phone interviews, 1996, 1997.

James Bailey, phone interview with author, 1997.

Charles Barber, phone interviews, 1996, 1997.

Roy Benner, letter to author, 1995.
Jack Blackwell, phone interviews, personal interviews, 1996, 1997.
Frank Buergler, phone interview with author, 1997.
James Chappelle, phone interviews, personal interviews, 1996, 1997.
William Coursey, phone interview with author, 1995.
Gunther Ctortnik, interview with author, 1997.
Phillip Dick, phone interview with author, letter to author, 1995.
Kenneth Duncan, phone interview with author, 1997.
Robert Emerick, letter to author, phone interview with author, 1996.
Welby Franz, phone interview with author, 1995.
Merle Gutherie, letter to author, phone interview with author, 1996.
Marvin Hall, phone interviews, personal interviews, 1996, 1997.
William Harnist, phone interviews, 1997.
Herman Heard, phone interviews, personal interviews, 1996, 1997.
Reskey Hibshman, letter to author, 1994.
Lee Holland, phone interview with author, 1997.
John Houston, phone interviews, 1998.
Philo Rockwell King III, letter to author, 1995.
Booker Nance, phone interview with author, 1995.
John O'Leary, phone interviews, 1996.
John Rearigh, letter to author, phone interview with author, 1996.
Washington Rector, phone interviews, 1995.
Fred Reese, phone interview with author, 1995.
Manuel Rogers, interview with author, 1998.
James Rookard, phone interviews, personal interviews, 1996, 1997.
Robert Rubino, personal interviews with author, 1997, 1998, 1999.
Fred Schlunz, letter to author, 1994.
John Shevlin, interview with author, 1995.
Charles Stevenson, phone interviews with author, 1995, 1996.
Earl Swallow, letter to author, 1995.
Charles Weko, phone interview with author, 1997.

David Colley served in the U.S. Army in 1963–64 with the Ordnance Corps. Formerly a reporter for the *Baltimore Evening Sun*, he is a freelance writer specializing in military affairs and history. Mr. Colley is the author of a previous book, *Soundwaves* (St. Martin's Press, 1985), and his work has appeared in the *New York Times*, *Popular Mechanics*, *Army*, *World War II*, *Mechanical Engineering*, and *Current Biography*. He contributed to *Faces of Victory*, a book on World War II published by the Veterans of Foreign Wars. His writing about the Red Ball Express in *World War II* received a Distinguished Article Award from the Army Historical Foundation. Mr. Colley lives in Easton, Pennsylvania.